MILESTONES
IN
AMERICAN HISTORY

THE UNDERGROUND RAILROAD

MILESTONES
IN
AMERICAN HISTORY

THE UNDERGROUND RAILROAD

THE JOURNEY TO FREEDOM

ANN MALASPINA

CHELSEA HOUSE
PUBLISHERS

An imprint of Infobase Publishing

The Underground Railroad

Chelsea House
An imprint of Infobase Publishing
132 West 31st Street
New York, NY 10001

Library of Congress Cataloging-in-Publication Data

Malaspina, Ann, 1957-
The Underground Railroad : the journey to freedom / by Ann Malaspina.
  p. cm.—(Milestones in American history)
Includes bibliographical references and index.
ISBN 978-1-60413-694-4 (hardcover)
1. Underground Railroad—Juvenile literature. 2. Slavery—United States—History—
Juvenile literature. 3. Fugitive slaves—United States—History—19th century—Juvenile
literature. 4. Antislavery movements—United States—History—19th century—Juvenile
literature. 5. Abolitionists—United States—History—19th century—Juvenile literature.
I. Title. II. Series.
E450.M26 2010
973.7'115—dc22   2009034815

Text design by Erik Lindstrom
Cover design by Alicia Post
Composition by Keith Trego
Cover printed by Bang Printing, Brainerd, MN
Book printed and bound by Bang Printing, Brainerd, MN
Date printed: January 2010
Printed in the United States of America

10 9 8 7 6 5 4 3 2 1

This book is printed on acid-free paper.

CONTENTS

Escaping the Lion's Den

The first time he planned to escape, Frederick Douglass was caught before he even left the farm where he worked. In 1835, Douglass and four other men decided to flee from slavery in Maryland. They hoped to paddle a canoe up the Chesapeake Bay and then walk to freedom in Pennsylvania. Someone must have informed on them because Douglass, who was about 17 years old, and the other men were tied up and dragged for miles behind a horse and cart, then thrown in a jail cell. Soon he was back in the hands of his owner, but Douglass would not give up his dream.

Born in 1818 to a slave mother and an unknown white father, Douglass had tasted freedom's possibilities. When he was a boy, the wife of one of his owners taught him the alphabet, until her husband found out and forbade her to educate

With help from a free black sailor—he used the seaman's iden-
tification papers and uniform—Frederick Douglass escaped
slavery in Maryland by boarding a train, a ferry, another train,
and a steamboat. He settled in New Bedford, Massachusetts,
and became a leader in the abolitionist movement. Pictured is
the cover of sheet music for "The Fugitive's Song," featuring
Douglass as a runaway slave.

the slave. With those few grains of knowledge, Douglass, whose mother died when he was young, taught himself to read and write. As a teenager, he was able to earn a small wage working on ships in the Baltimore Harbor, but he knew that his future was limited. He was sent to work for different farmers—one of them a slave-breaker who beat Douglass for letting the oxen loose. "I was fast approaching manhood, and year after year had passed, and I was still a slave,"[1] he recalled.

CIVIL DISOBEDIENCE

Around the time of Douglass's failed escape, a loosely organized effort to help African-American slaves escape to freedom was growing stronger. It was called the Underground Railroad after the cast-iron rails being laid across the country. An informal network of people and safe houses that helped fugitive slaves pass over the borders to freedom in the Northern states and Canada, this railroad was not run by steam engines or carried by iron wheels, nor did it have permanent tracks or scheduled stops. Yet it successfully moved people through Kentucky and Virginia, Ohio and Indiana, and spanned from Maryland to Pennsylvania, New York, Massachusetts, Vermont, and finally into Canada, where even the harshest fugitive slave laws could not reach. Runaway slaves traveled any way they could—on steamships, railroads, riverboats, wagons, horses, and foot—as they crossed rivers, waded into swamps, ran across fields and through woods, and tried to pass invisibly through the cities of Baltimore, Louisville, and Norfolk. They endured freezing weather, hunger, fear, and other terrible hardships on their way north. Few official records were kept of the slaves who fled from their owners. Many who escaped were later captured, and fewer still made it safely to freedom. Most slaves did not run from their owners. Yet historians estimate that tens of thousands of slaves may have escaped, sometimes with help from free blacks, other slaves, and white abolitionists, between 1820 and 1865, when the Thirteenth Amendment to the Constitution finally ended slavery.

In defying the laws of slavery, the fugitives and their helpers were staging a revolution and a protest against an institution that seemed, until then, impossible to eradicate. For more than 200 years, the free labor of slaves had helped to build a new country and keep it growing. Slaves plowed fields, planted and picked crops, built fences, shod horses, washed dirty laundry, babysat children, cooked meals, and even helped construct the White House. Slavery was legal in all 13 original colonies and accepted by the majority of the early settlers.

After the American Revolution, Eli Whitney's patenting of the cotton gin in 1793 made the expansion of American slavery inevitable. With Whitney's new device to remove the seeds from the cotton fiber, a process once done laboriously by hand, Southern planters could suddenly process more cotton, and so they quickly expanded their fields. They still needed slaves to do the planting and harvesting, and with larger crops, they needed many more. By the 1850s, three-quarters of the world's cotton was grown in America. Once harvested, it was made into cotton cloth in mills in England and New England. Cotton was the country's most important export, and it depended on the aching backs and sore hands of slaves.

PROPERTY, NOT PEOPLE

Slave owners insisted that slaves were property, not people. They believed, or at least pretended to believe, that their slaves were willing and even grateful and that they did not want or need freedom. The idea that slaves wanted to be free was a threat to the slaveholders' way of life and beliefs. As one slave owner wrote in a Virginia newspaper in 1859, "While the crazy fanatics of the North imagine that the poor negro, smarting under a galling sense of his degradation, and inspired by a noble impulse of resistance to tyranny, is ready at a moment's warning to grasp the murderous pike and fight for his freedom, the people of the South feel the most perfect security in the full assurance that they possess not only the willing obedience but the strong attachment of their slaves."[2] Even Northern states like New York and Massachusetts, where slavery had been outlawed, relied on and profited from trade with the slave states. While many Northerners did not favor enslaving other humans, they were not ready to push for change in the status quo. Yet an undercurrent of disgust with slavery was building.

The Underground Railroad gained steam with the abolitionist movement, a reform and protest crusade that worked toward a final end to slavery. On January 1, 1831, William Lloyd Garrison called for the immediate and complete emancipation of all slaves in the first issue of his antislavery newspaper, *The Liberator*. Garrison and other abolitionists looked at slavery as a moral evil that needed to be wiped away. They were willing to do anything, including break the law, to make it happen. They formed antislavery organizations and vigilance committees, published newspapers, held rallies, and petitioned Congress to outlaw slavery. Many abolitionists also joined the Underground Railroad, opening their homes, pockets, and hearts to help runaway slaves. "The only free road, the Underground Railroad, is owned and managed by the Vigilant Committee. They have tunneled under the whole breadth of the land,"[3] the writer and philosopher Henry David Thoreau said in a speech in 1859 in Concord, Massachusetts.

Many people, both black and white, contributed to the Underground Railroad. "It was the country's first racially integrated civil rights movement, in which whites and blacks worked together,"[4] Fergus M. Bordewich writes in his book, *Bound for Canaan: The Underground Railroad and the War for the Soul of America*. There was Thomas Garrett, a Quaker store owner in Wilmington, Delaware, who gave money and safe passage to hundreds of runaway slaves. John Parker, a freed black man in Ripley, Ohio, owned an iron foundry and helped many slaves navigate their way to freedom. Isaac A. Flint was a white man who posed as a slave buyer and bought Samuel Burris his freedom on the auction block in Dover, Delaware.

It was hard for runaway slaves to know who could be trusted. Black and white abolitionists risked serious punishment to do what was right. Here, a plantation school teacher offers help to a slave in the 1850s.

Burris was a free black who had been caught helping slaves escape from Delaware and Maryland and was about to be sold into slavery. While some devoted their lives to helping free the slaves, others just happened to be there when a runaway slave needed assistance.

The many black men and women, both freed and enslaved, who made freedom possible for others, have often been over-looked. Historians now believe that they were the most impor-tant link in the Underground Railroad. Only a handful of them are famous, such as Harriet Tubman, the Maryland field slave who led dozens of people to freedom. Even Tubman relied on others to get to "the Promised Land," as slaves called the free states and Canada. One winter night, Tubman's father, who by then had been freed and was working on the Underground

Railroad, risked losing his liberty to help his daughter get several of her brothers out of Maryland.

"SORROWS OF HIS HEART"

Like tens of thousands of American slaves, Frederick Augustus Washington Bailey, as Douglass was originally named, experienced extreme hardship. He slept on nothing but the hard ground, worked in winter without a coat or shoes, and was whipped by his owners. When he was a child, he ate from a trough with the other young slaves on the plantation. Douglass would later describe slavery as a life of humiliation, sweat, blood, boredom, and lost opportunities. If people thought that slaves' songs expressed joy or happiness, they were wrong, Douglass wrote in his autobiography *Narrative of the Life of Frederick Douglass.* "Slaves sing most when they are most unhappy. The songs of the slave represent the sorrows of his heart."[5]

Such a grim life gave Douglass the desire and courage to risk everything for freedom. When an opportunity to escape came again, in 1838, Douglass succeeded in fleeing north with the help of the Underground Railroad. He was disguised as a sailor, and a friend had lent him "free papers" identifying him as a free man. Douglass got to Philadelphia and then boarded a train to New York City.

When he finally disembarked in New York, he was relieved and joyful at the same time. "Here I am, in the great city of New York, safe and sound, without loss of blood or bone. . . . A free state around me, and a free earth under my feet! What a moment was this to me! A whole year was pressed into a single day. A new world burst upon my agitated vision."[6] He made contact with the antislavery leader David Ruggles, who ran the New York Committee of Vigilance that helped protect fugitive slaves. Ruggles let Douglass stay at his house at 36 Lispenard Street, a safe house on the Underground Railroad. In fact, Douglass never provided details of his escape or named those who helped him. He could not understand why people revealed information about their escapes and who had helped them. He did not want to "run the hazard of closing the slightest avenue by which a brother slave might clear himself of the chains and fetters of slavery."[7]

When fugitive slaves finally reached the free states, they faced another difficult journey. Often this was when the Underground Railroad helped the most. Alone and often without resources, the fugitives needed to start a new life. Upon arriving in New York, Douglass wrote, "I felt like one who had escaped a den of hungry lions. This state of mind, however, very soon subsided; and I was again seized with a feeling of great insecurity and loneliness. I was yet liable to be taken back, and subjected to all the tortures of slavery. . . . But the loneliness overcame me. There I was in the midst of thousands, and yet a perfect stranger; without home and without friends, in the midst of thousands of my own brethren—children of a com mon Father, and yet I dared not to unfold to any one of them my sad condition."[8] Slave catchers roamed the streets of New York, so Douglass was not truly safe there, either. If he were caught, fugitive slave laws required his return to his owner. Ruggles helped him move on to the port city of New Bedford, Massachusetts, where a free black family gave him and his new wife, Anna, a room. Douglass went to work as a caulker on the boats in the harbor. Like many fugitive slaves, the chance to work and earn a living was the key to real freedom.

Soon after, Douglass began to speak out against slavery. People listened to the tall, powerfully built man with a handsome face who spoke eloquently and with force. In freedom, Douglass became a popular leader in the antislavery movement. A celebrated writer, Douglass published the antislavery newspaper *The North Star*. He moved to Rochester, New York, where his home was a safe house for fugitive slaves. Just as Ruggles and others had helped him on his way to freedom, Douglass would spend the rest of his life extending his hand and his voice to the slaves still living in chains.

Liberty to All

The history of the Underground Railroad began on the shores of West Africa, where European slave traders sank their anchors and loaded up on human cargo. As early as the 1400s, Portuguese merchants captured Africans to sell as slaves in Europe. Some were already slaves in Africa, and African traders bartered with the Europeans over the human goods. In the 1500s, Spanish ships began to carry African slaves to the Americas, launching the transatlantic slave trade. The lucrative business developed as a triangular economy. European traders brought goods to West Africa to sell for slaves. They transported the slaves to the Americas and sold them for profits. The slaves were put to work in the sugar, tobacco, and cotton fields. The traders exported the commodities back to Europe for more profits, enabling them to buy and sell more goods and slaves.

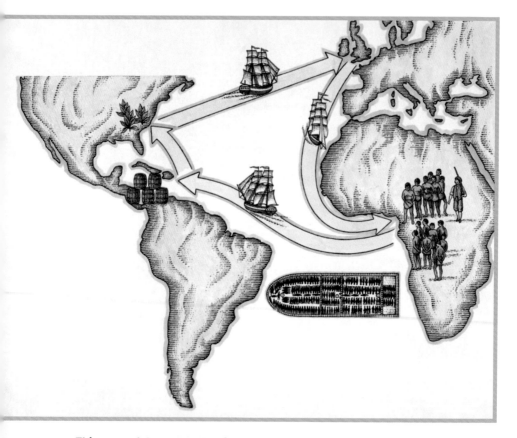

This map of the transatlantic slave trade shows the principal trade routes of the slave ships. The routes form a triangle between merchants in Great Britain, slaves in West Africa, goods in the Caribbean, and tobacco leaves in North America.

European schooners were soon hauling tens of thousands of Africans to labor on the Caribbean sugar plantations, Virginia tobacco fields, and the small farms and growing cities of New England. By the late 1700s, the British were the most active in the slave trade. Historians estimate that 11 million slaves may have been transported across the Atlantic during the international slave trade. Some one million Africans died during the voyage, known as the Middle Passage, from the inhumane conditions on the boats. Olaudah Equiano, an African who wrote a narrative of his life, tells of his journey on a slave ship:

The closeness of the place, and the heat of the climate, added to the number in the ship, which was so crowded that each had scarcely room to turn himself, almost suffocated us. This produced copious perspirations, so that the air soon became unfit for respiration, from a variety of loathsome smells, and brought on a sickness among the slaves, of which many died. . . . This wretched situation was again aggravated by the galling of the chains . . . and the filth of the necessary tubs, into which the children often fell, and were almost suffocated. The shrieks of the women, and the groans of the dying, rendered the whole a scene of horror almost inconceivable.[1]

Only a few of the horrors were documented, such as this one: In the 1780s, the captain of the slave ship *Zong* threw 132 sick and weak Africans overboard in the hopes of collecting insurance payments.

FIRST AFRICANS IN AMERICA

In 1565, the Spanish established their first permanent colonial settlement in Florida. African slaves from Cuba were brought over to build the fort in St. Augustine. They constructed buildings and bridges and worked in the fields and mines. In 1619, a group of Africans carried on a Dutch slave ship was deposited in Jamestown, the first permanent English settlement, located in present-day Virginia. The 20 Africans were probably indentured servants. After they worked for four to seven years without pay, they would be set free.

Jamestown soon needed more workers for a thriving tobacco industry. Tobacco was first planted on the fertile coastal land in 1612. The colonists discovered that tobacco grew well and was easy to ship to England, where it was in high demand. By 1619, Jamestown was exporting tons of tobacco every year, but it took intensive labor to plant and harvest the valuable crop. The settlers realized that slaves were more cost-efficient than indentured servants. Though white men and women worked as indentured servants to pay off their transport from

England, only blacks and sometimes Native Americans wound up as slaves. Because of the labor demands of tobacco and other large-scale agricultural crops like rice and cotton grown in warmer climates, colonists in the South grew more dependent upon slave labor than those in the North, but slavery was soon widespread throughout the New World.

In 1641, Massachusetts was the first colony to formally legalize slavery when it passed the Massachusetts Body of Liberties, the first legal code in the colonies. The code included the following passage:

> There shall never be any bond slavery, villeinage, or captivity amongst us unless it be lawful captives taken in just wars, and such strangers as willingly sell themselves or are sold to us. And these shall have all the liberties and Christian usages which the law of God established in Israel concerning such persons doth morally require. This exempts none from servitude who shall be judged thereto by authority.[2]

Other colonies followed, weaving slavery into the social fabric and economy of colonial America. By 1760, there were some 200,000 slaves in the American colonies. They worked in coal mines in Kentucky, on steamboats in the Mississippi, as blacksmiths in Virginia, and as lumberjacks in Maryland and Georgia. On average, slaves worked 14- to 18-hour days.

"THE LAW OF GOD"

Slavery was allowed to take root because of the religious and social attitudes of the early colonists. The pioneering settlers were Puritans and other fundamentalist Protestants who sought a new start in life after being persecuted in England. They had crossed the ocean in search of religious freedom, yet they justified slavery through their religious views. They believed that God had selected them for a purpose and that blacks were inferior and less than human, fated to be servants

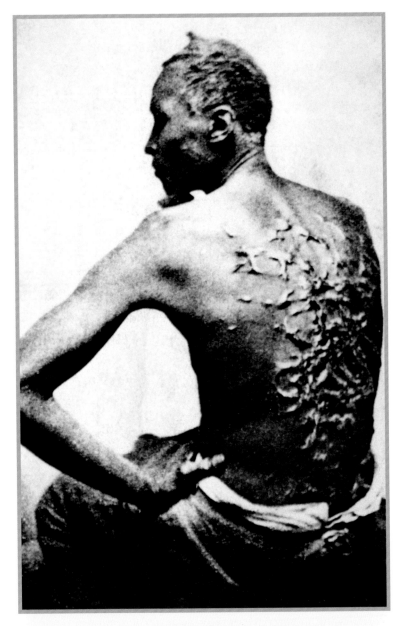

Gordon, a freed slave in Baton Rouge, Louisiana, displays his whip-scarred back on April 2, 1863. Slaves had no protection or recourse from the harsh treatment of their overseers. Punishment for some of the smallest misdemeanors included whipping, mutilating, branding, and other various instruments of torture.

to whites. Puritan leader Cotton Mather wrote in 1693 that blacks were enslaved because they had sinned against God, and he urged them to go to church. The 1641 Massachusetts law that allowed slavery referred to "the law of God." Yet slavery then and later was primarily an answer to labor shortages and economic demands.

Because slaves were not considered to be human, their owners could think of them instead as chattel, or property, to buy and sell. In addition, slaves shared few of the rights of white people. This arrangement worked well for the white colonists, determined to make a good living and prosper in their new land. They did not have to shoulder the cost of providing slaves with education and decent shelter and clothing. Slave children often were not given pants to wear for several years. Nor were slaves allowed to rebel or protest their treatment, or in any way assert their rights. They had no recourse if mistreated. William Wells Brown, born a slave in Kentucky, describes the terror that slaves often had to endure in his autobiography, *Narrative of William W. Brown, a Fugitive Slave*:

> My mother was a field hand, and one morning was ten or fifteen minutes behind the others in getting into the field. As soon as she reached the spot where they were at work, the overseer commenced whipping her. She cried, "Oh! pray—Oh! pray—Oh! Pray"—these are generally the words of slaves, when imploring mercy at the hands of their oppressors. I heard her voice, and knew it, and jumped out of my bunk, and went to the door. Though the field was some distance from the house, I could hear every crack of the whip, and every groan and cry of my poor mother. . . . It was not yet daylight.[3]

EARLY QUESTS FOR FREEDOM

Even in the early years of the colonies, slaves were trying to get free. "The desire for freedom was in the mind of nearly every enslaved negro. Liberty was the subject of the dreams and visions of slave preachers and sibyls; it was the object of their prayers,"[4] writes Wilbur H. Siebert, an early scholar of the Underground Railroad. By the mid-1700s, slaves were fleeing their masters in sizable numbers, but it was not an easy feat. Rarely were they able to get very far. Slaves in the Southern colonies of Georgia and the Carolinas were sometimes more fortunate because the Spanish colony of Florida was not so far away.

The Florida peninsula was a haven for runaway slaves. The Spanish who colonized the region had a different attitude toward slavery from what the British had. They believed that slavery was a temporary condition and that people should be able to work their way out of it. In October 1687, 11 runaway slaves from Charleston, South Carolina (then known as Charles Town), fled to Florida. They arrived by boat, and Governor Quiroga, the Spanish ruler, gave them refuge in St. Augustine. The Africans were baptized by a Catholic priest and given housing. They were also given work as blacksmiths, cooks, and laundry workers—and they were paid. An official from Charles Town tried to get the slaves back, but Governor Quiroga insisted they remain free.

In 1693, the Spanish king, Charles II, proclaimed that English slaves who came to Spanish territory would be given their freedom. He was "giving liberty to all . . . the men as well as the women . . . so that by their example and by my liberality others will do the same."[5] Not all Spanish leaders were so enlightened. Later rulers tried to profit by selling slaves back to their English owners, and one instituted a mandatory four-year military service for slaves to gain their liberty. Mostly, though, the fugitives were baptized Catholic and given work. The Florida sanctuary did not last forever. In 1763, the Treaty of Paris, which ended the Seven Years' War in Europe, gave Florida to Great Britain in return for Spain gaining control of Havana, Cuba. The Spanish and many African residents left Florida for

Cuba. British investors cleared the land for plantations and imported Africans across the Atlantic Ocean for slave labor. At the end of the Revolutionary War, Spain regained control of Florida. Runaways once again fled from Georgia and the Carolinas to claim freedom. But the new United States government was not happy about the situation.

The Spanish ended the sanctuary policy by 1790. African slaves who ran to Florida were still able to settle alongside the

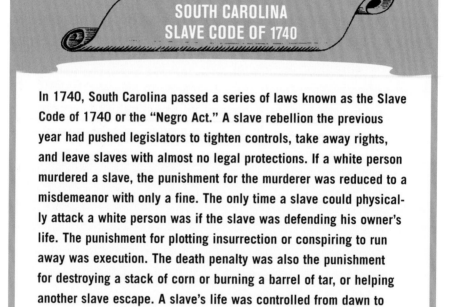

SOUTH CAROLINA SLAVE CODE OF 1740

In 1740, South Carolina passed a series of laws known as the Slave Code of 1740 or the "Negro Act." A slave rebellion the previous year had pushed legislators to tighten controls, take away rights, and leave slaves with almost no legal protections. If a white person murdered a slave, the punishment for the murderer was reduced to a misdemeanor with only a fine. The only time a slave could physically attack a white person was if the slave was defending his owner's life. The punishment for plotting insurrection or conspiring to run away was execution. The death penalty was also the punishment for destroying a stack of corn or burning a barrel of tar, or helping another slave escape. A slave's life was controlled from dawn to dusk. Under the new laws, they were not allowed to grow their own food. Even their clothes could be made only from certain coarse fabrics. Slaves could not learn to read or write, or assemble with other slaves. If they did, they would be flogged. This code remained in effect until 1865. Following is an excerpt from the code:

XVII. Any slave who shall be guilty of homicide of any sort, upon any white person, except by misadventure or in defence of his master or other person under whose care and government such slave shall be, shall upon conviction thereof as aforesaid, suf-

Seminole Indians in the interior of mid-Florida. The Africans were given land in return for giving part of their crops to the Seminoles. Soon the two groups began to intermarry. This era, too, came to an end. In 1821, Florida became a territory of the United States. Andrew Jackson, the new Florida governor, decided to remove Seminoles and free blacks from the Florida peninsula to make way for white settlers. A tragic chapter in American history unfolded when the Seminoles and Africans

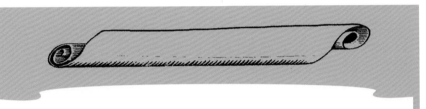

fer death. And every slave who shall raise or attempt to raise an insurrection in this Province, or shall endeavor to delude or entice any slave to run away and leave this Province; every such slave and slaves, and his and their accomplices, aiders and abettors, shall upon conviction as aforesaid suffer death. Provided always, [t]hat it shall and may be lawful to and for the justices who shall pronounce sentence against such slaves, and by and with the advice and consent of the freeholders as aforesaid, if several slaves shall receive sentence at one time, to mitigate and alter the sentence of any slave other than such as shall be convicted of the homicide of a white person, who they shall think may deserve mercy, and may inflict such corporal punishment (other than death) on any such slave, as they in their discretion shall think fit, any thing herein contained to the contrary thereof in any wise notwithstanding. Provided, [t]hat one or more of the said slaves who shall be convicted of the crimes or offences aforesaid, where several are concerned, shall be executed for example, to deter others from offending in the like kind.*

*"South Carolina Slave Code of 1740." Available online. URL: http://law.jrank.org/pages/11669/South-Carolina-Slave-Code-South-Carolina-Slave-Code.html.

were forced on a long walk west to Indian Territory, leaving Florida for whites.

Even before the American Revolution, the fear of slaves running off led the colonies to take action. Slave codes, or laws governing slaves, were enacted to discourage slaves from trying to escape. A slave who was found away from his or her master's property could be killed under South Carolina's 1740 slave code. Georgia also permitted slave catchers to kill adult male slaves who ran away. The state's 1755 slave code provided a larger reward for retrieving a dead male slave than for returning a live woman or child.

Owners wanted full control of their slaves, and the laws and courts backed them most of the time. In 1829, the North Carolina Supreme Court took up a case concerning a slave named Lydia who was hired out to work for John Mann. When she tried to escape from a whipping, Mann shot and wounded her. Mann was found guilty and received a $5 fine in the local court, but the higher court overturned his conviction. "The power of the master must be absolute, to render the submission of the slave perfect," wrote North Carolina Chief Justice Thomas Ruffin in *State v. Mann*.[6]

Slave codes did not quell the fear of insurrection among slave owners nor discourage slaves from rebelling. The case of a slave who fled his British "master" led to upheaval among slaves in the American colonies. The slave, James Somersett, had been taken to England by his owner. He ran away but was captured, put in chains, and sent on a ship to Jamaica. Somersett sued for his freedom. In 1772, the British chief justice Lord Mansfield said that slavery was "so odious, that nothing can be suffered to support it, but positive law."[7] He ruled that Somersett be set free because England neither allowed nor approved of slavery. Mansfield's ruling made slavery illegal in England, but did not outlaw the practice in the American colonies. The news made American slaves even more restless and determined for change. Several slaves unsuccessfully petitioned the courts for freedom, saying that Lord Mansfield's decision should apply to the colonies.

LORD DUNMORE'S PROCLAMATION

When the Revolutionary War broke out in 1775, many slaves felt that their fate would be best tied to the British. If the British won the war, the slaves thought they were more likely to be freed.

Lord Dunmore, the Royal Governor of Virginia, turned to recruiting slaves to expand his army. In 1775, he issued a proclamation, offering freedom to any slave who joined his so-called Ethiopian Regiment. He stated: "And I hereby further declare all indentured servants, Negroes, or others (appertaining to Rebels) free, that are able and willing to bear arms, they joining His Majesty's Troops, as soon as may be, for the more speedily reducing the Colony to a proper sense of their duty, to this Majesty's crown and dignity."[8]

Lord Dunmore soon had 800 men in his regiment, but he had also raised the ire of the Virginia slaveholders, who feared they would not only lose their slaves but also face an uprising. Some historians consider Lord Dunmore's proclamation as the first significant emancipation of slaves in American history— yet it came with a big price. The Virginia legislature quickly passed a new law that set the death penalty as punishment for any slave who escaped from his owner.

Fugitive and freed slaves also tried to join the Continental Army. At first, General George Washington, commander-in-chief of the army, did not allow black soldiers, particularly slaves, whom he believed were not fit to be soldiers. After all, he was a slaveholder and owned more than 300 slaves at Mount Vernon, his plantation in Virginia. Washington needed more men for his ragged Continental Army, however. He realized that black soldiers could help the colonists' cause and finally allowed them to fight. Many black soldiers fought in the American Revolution on both sides. Some 100,000 slaves escaped during the Revolution; many fled north to Canada or free states, while others joined the army.

A NEW SLAVE NATION

The Revolutionary War between Great Britain and the American colonies ended with the colonists' victory in 1783. Now the colonists had to create a new frame of government, a process that would take several years. Fifty-five delegates, representing the 13 original colonies, met at the Constitutional Convention in Philadelphia in May 1787. As debate got under way over the Constitution, the issue of slavery was contentious. Some delegates, like Thomas Jefferson, wanted to stop the spread of slavery and the international slave trade, but most agreed that the right of a slaveholder to own slaves was a basic property right and should not be taken away.

Slavery was legal in most of the states but it was far less common in the North. By 1787, slaves made up one-fifth of the national population, but comprised about 40 percent of the population in the South. South Carolina and other Southern states wanted slaves to be counted as people to increase their representation in Congress, and as property when the federal government taxed states according to population. Northern states, where slavery was not as prevalent, wanted the opposite. A compromise was finally reached, known as the Three-Fifths Compromise. Slaves would be counted as three-fifths of a person in terms of both taxation and representation in the House of Representatives. The delegates also debated whether to stop the importation of African slaves, but South Carolina and Georgia threatened not to join the Union if that happened. Instead, the delegates allowed the slave trade to continue until 1808. Creating a new nation that was united was more important to the delegates than the issue of slavery.

The Constitution confirmed the continuation of slavery by including the so-called "fugitive slave and felon clause." Article IV, clause 2, of the Constitution stated:

No person held to service or labor in one state, under the laws thereof, escaping into another, shall, in consequence of any law or regulation therein, be discharged from such service or labor, but shall be delivered up on claim of the party to whom such service or labor may be due.[9]

This clause made it legal for fugitive slaves to be returned to their owners. In fact, people in non-slave states often refused to return runaways, and federal enforcement of this clause remained vague. Even so, Canada became a destination for runaways by the end of the 1700s.

As the Constitution indicated, the nation's founders advocated the principles of freedom and democracy, but not when it came to slaves. Many of the Founding Fathers, such as Jefferson and Washington, had grown up with slavery and owned many slaves. Though Jefferson and Washington were ambivalent about slavery, and at times spoke against it, they did not want to abolish it. The outspoken antislavery proponent, John Adams of Boston, who would become Washington's vice president and then the second president of the United States, was an exception among his peers. His wife, Abigail, also opposed slavery and hired only freed blacks as servants.

FUGITIVE SLAVE ACT OF 1793

Yet, after the Revolution, the spirit of egalitarianism and liberty had turned more people against slavery. While the federal government tried to enforce its fugitive slave law, the Northern states began to abolish slavery. The fact that slavery was still prevalent in much of the country, and would greatly expand with the new cotton gin in the Southern states, led to a growing rift in the new nation. In the early 1790s, a fugitive slave from Virginia caused a furor between states and led to a crackdown on runaway slaves. John Davis ran from his master and fled over the state border to Pennsylvania, which was by then a free state. Three lawmen caught Davis in Pennsylvania and brought him back to Virginia. Governor Thomas Mifflin of Pennsylvania was angry; he considered Davis to be a freed man and safe from capture in his state. He tried to extradite the three slave catchers to Pennsylvania, but the Virginia governor refused to comply. In response, Congress drafted the Fugitive Slave Act that took away rights, not just from slaves, but from freed slaves, as well.

The 1793 law was an attempt to balance the property rights of slave states with the guarantees of civil liberties in the free states. It also reinforced the fugitive slave clause in the Constitution. Runaway slaves could no longer expect to live freely even in states that had outlawed slavery. The law allowed a slave's owner or a professional slave catcher to capture runaways in free states. The slave catchers often used bloodhounds, known as "Negro dogs," specially trained to follow the human scent. Slave catchers could make as much as $600 a year trailing and catching fugitive slaves, sometimes bringing the wrong person back to the owner—but one slave was as good as another, according to some.

The captured person would be forced to confess that he belonged to that owner. Others helped the slave catchers, including local sheriffs, slave owners, and just ordinary people who felt they should be law-abiding. The law also took away rights of citizenship from runaway slaves in free states. Treated as property, they did not have a right to due process, or other formal legal proceedings, such as a right to a lawyer or a trial by jury. The slave catcher only had to say orally to a state or federal judge that the captured person was a runaway slave. In addition, people who took in an escaped slave could be fined $500. Thus the Quakers and others who helped runaway slaves faced stiff penalties, but many states did not abide by the law. Northern states passed laws that guaranteed trials by jury and other protections for fugitive slaves who were caught, thus virtually ignoring the federal law.

Escaped slaves would hide in the woods and in swamps during the day and travel at night. They subsisted on wild fruit they would gather, crossing rivers and passing over hills they did not know, facing danger at every turn. Slaveowners would hunt for them using bloodhounds, and within a few days most runaways were brought back to the plantation and severely punished.

SLAVE REVOLTS

Also in the 1790s, news of a violent slave revolt in the Caribbean stirred fear among slave owners. The revolt occurred in Saint-Domingue, a prosperous French colony on the island of Hispaniola that produced 40 percent of the world's sugar on its cane plantations. The arduous work of planting and cutting sugar cane in the tropical heat was done by tens of thousands of African slaves. Because of the labor-intensive economy, slaves outnumbered the white colonists. Led by a slave named Toussaint L'Ouverture, the bloody revolt lasted from 1791 to 1804 and ended with the expulsion of the white slave owners. The colony was renamed Haiti and became the first free black republic in the world. Such an event was unprecedented and led many slave owners to wonder if a similar revolution could occur in the United States.

One of the first major slave revolts planned in the South was led by Gabriel Prosser, a 24-year-old slave whose outrage at slavery was fueled by his deeply held Christian beliefs. He plotted to take over the city of Richmond, Virginia, in the summer of 1800 and to arm rebel slaves with artillery stolen from the federal armory there. He gathered the support of thousands of slaves and stockpiled guns, but two followers betrayed him. To add to the obstacles, the day that the revolt was planned, a flood destroyed the bridges leading into Richmond. Prosser was caught and later hung, along with some of his followers. Though Prosser was unable to carry out his plans, slave owners were astonished that he had nearly taken over a major city.

THE QUAKERS

In the late 1700s, people began to make concerted efforts to help fugitive slaves gain freedom. One of the first groups to do so was the Quakers. These members of a radical Christian sect had suffered persecution in England. A young Quaker, William Penn, was expelled from Oxford University for his beliefs. In search of religious freedom, and backed by his wealthy family,

Penn founded the colony of Pennsylvania in 1682. Pennsylvania and its capital city, Philadelphia, became home to a growing number of Quakers. Early Quaker settlers did not necessarily oppose slavery, and Penn himself owned slaves. Yet the Pennsylvania economy, with its small farms and industries, never came to rely on slave labor. Also, Quaker beliefs supported the notion of equality and freedom for all people.

As early as 1688, the Quakers of Germantown, Pennsylvania, protested, "And those who steal or rob men, and those who buy or purchase them, are they not all alike?"[10] Over the next two centuries, many Quakers did whatever possible to help slaves reach freedom. In 1775, a group of Philadelphia Quakers, along with Benjamin Franklin, founded The Pennsylvanian Society for the Relief of Free Negroes Unlawfully Held in Bondage. Later called the Pennsylvania Abolition Society, it was the first antislavery organization in the colonies. Quakers also started schools for black children. In 1780, Pennsylvania passed an act for the gradual abolition of slavery.

One Pennsylvania Quaker in particular was willing to risk everything to help fugitives. Isaac T. Hopper was born in 1771 and later converted to Quakerism. In 1796, he was elected to the Pennsylvania Abolition Society. He taught at schools for black children and adults. Soon he was helping blacks who claimed to have been kidnapped or mistaken for slaves, as well as real fugitives, get free from captivity. He and his friends began to reach out to farmers, Quakers, and other antislavery sympathizers, both black and white, to help runaway slaves in and around Philadelphia. For his tireless efforts, some people would call him the Father of the Underground Railroad. As Fergus M. Bordewich writes in *Bound for Canaan*, "He probably never imagined that the underground that he was inventing would eventually extend its reach across every Northern state, and that it would help bring the nation to the brink of Civil War."[11]

House on Fire

In 1831, a slave named Tice Davids from Maysville, Kentucky, ran off from his master. He headed for the Ohio River, which marked the border between the slave state of Kentucky and the free state of Ohio. Davids might have swum across the river, while his owner borrowed a small skiff to chase after him. Once on the far bank, the owner could find no sign of his escaped property. Somehow Davids had disappeared, probably with the help of others ready to hide him away to safety. Frustrated, the man is said to have declared that Davids must have "gone off on an underground road."[1]

In the 1830s, people began using the words *Underground Railroad* to describe the increasingly organized effort to help fugitive slaves on their journeys to freedom. The phrase reflected the advent of the steam railroad, a revolutionary industrial development of that decade. "Railroad fever" swept

with the eastern boundary line of the state o

from it, and took its rise from two lesser pat

verged at

either sid

line. The

dle route

three br

crossed th

son, New

neighborh

worth, p

through I

Loganspoi

Michigan

of Lake N

third or

followed

River   to

where   it

river, proc

selaer, and

easterly to

line, maki

to Michig

where the

entered th

Bormay & Co., N. Y.

Well-known routes. Routes not well established.

ROUTES THROUGH INDIANA AND MICHIGAN
IN 1848.

As traced by Lewis Falley.

the two crossing-places on the Michigan bord

This page from Wilbur Siebert's *The Underground Railroad from Slavery to Freedom*, published in 1899, shows the routes through Indiana and Michigan in 1848 used by runaway slaves.

the nation as the Baltimore & Ohio Railroad began to operate the first passenger trains on newly laid rails starting in Baltimore in 1830. Soon, railroad tracks were opening up the East Coast to transportation and linking major cities, before expanding westward across the country. The railroad changed the ways that people traveled and goods were transported, and it helped build the economy with faster trade and communication. Like the new railroad tracks, the clandestine routes of the Underground Railroad crisscrossed the nation, connecting people and places in ways that had never been done before.

A NEW LANGUAGE

To protect the runaways, the Underground Railroad had its own language and ways of communicating. In Harrison County, Ohio, three knocks on a door meant that fugitives were waiting outside. "To the inquiry, 'Who's there?' the reply was, "A friend with friends,'"[2] the historian Wilbur Siebert recounts. Canada was called "heaven" or "the Promised Land," while slave states were called "Egypt," the biblical land where slaves were kept, and "loads of potatoes" or "parcels of wood" referred to groups of fugitive slaves. But after the 1830s, a railroad vocabulary was introduced, including words such as *train conductor, engine, passengers*, and *stations*. The fugitive slaves and abolitionists used railroad terms to identify the people and places that helped the runaways on their harrowing travels. They could say the common railroad words in public, without revealing that they were talking about breaking the law. The word *underground* indicated that all the travel on this particular railroad had to be done in deep secrecy, often at night or in obscurity.

Soon people who helped the slaves were sprinkling railroad words into their everyday conversations. Levi Coffin, a Quaker "conductor" in Newport, Indiana, is thought to have aided thousands of fugitives on their way to freedom. He owned a store that sold goods made by freed slaves and a house that was nicknamed Grand Central Station, after the busy railroad station in New York City. Later, Coffin wrote a book about his experiences, often using railroad terms to refer to his work. After 19 slaves arrived at his house one day, he told the men helping them that they were "about as many as the cars can bear at one time. Now you may switch off and put your locomotives in my stable and let them blow off steam, and we will water and feed them."[3]

Runaway slaves, too, knew that by using the code words to describe their journeys, they were helping to remain safe. A person who coordinated the slaves' passage was called an "agent." An alternate escape route was called a "bypass" or "runaround." "Brakemen" made contacts for runaway slaves, while a "conductor" or "operator" or "agent" helped the slaves escape. A "station" was a safe place where fugitive slaves could hide. People who were in charge of a "station" were called "station masters." A "stockholder" helped to donate food, money, and clothing. And runaway slaves were referred to as "passengers" or sometimes "baggage." Other terms were also used.

"FLOGGED UP"

Slaves had many reasons to try to escape. Some wanted to join husbands, wives, children, or parents who had already left for a free state. Others dreamed of freedom and the chance to set their own course in life. Once Frederick Douglass moved from a Maryland farm to the city of Baltimore when he was about 12 years old and saw what freedom might hold for him, he could not stop thinking about it: "The silver trump of freedom had roused my soul to eternal wakefulness. Freedom now appeared, to disappear no more forever. It was heard in every sound, and seen in every thing,"[4] he recalled.

For some slaves, the fear of being sold away from their families made them decide to run. After the international

(continues on page 32)

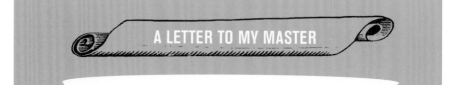

Henry Bibb was born on May 10, 1815, to Mildred Jackson, a slave on William Gatewood's plantation in Shelby County, Kentucky. People told him that his father was James Bibb, a state senator from Kentucky, whom he never met. His six younger brothers were sold away, and he grew up working on the farm. He married another mixed-race slave in 1833, and they had a daughter. Bibb had always wanted his freedom. He escaped once, but when he returned to get his family, he was captured. He finally fled to Detroit in 1842, leaving behind his wife and daughter.

Bibb joined the abolitionist movement, traveling around the United States and speaking about his experiences as a slave. He gained fame after he wrote his autobiography, *Narrative of the Life and Adventures of Henry Bibb, An American Slave, Written by Himself*, in 1849. Bibb and his second wife, Mary Miles, moved to Ontario, Canada, to escape capture under the Fugitive Slave Act of 1850. There he joined the black abolitionist Josiah Henson and they formed the Refugees' Home Colony in Sandwich Township for escaped slaves. Bibb started a famous antislavery newspaper, *Voice of the Fugitive*. Earlier, soon after his escape from slavery, Bibb wrote a letter to his former owner. It is astonishing for its honesty and frankness. In freedom, he was able to say all that he could not as a slave:

> March 23, 1844 Detroit
> Dear Sir:—I am happy to inform you that you are not mistaken in the man whom you sold as property, and received pay for as such. But I thank God that I am not property now, but am regarded as a man like yourself, and although I live far north, I am enjoying a comfortable living by my own industry. If you should

ever chance to be traveling this way, and will call on me, I will use you better than you did me while you held me as a slave. Think not that I have any malice against you, for the cruel treatment which you inflicted on me while I was in your power. As it was the custom of your country, to treat your fellow men as you did me and my little family, I can freely forgive you. . . .

You may perhaps think hard of us for running away from slavery, but as to myself, I have but one apology to make for it, which is this: I have only to regret that I did not start at an earlier period. I might have been free long before I was. But you had it in your power to have kept me there much longer than you did. I think it is very probable that I should have been a toiling slave on your plantation today, if you had treated me differently.

To be compelled to stand by and see you whip and slash my wife without mercy, when I could afford her no protection, not even by offering myself to suffer the lash in her place, was more than I felt it to be the duty of a slave husband to endure, while the way was open to Canada. My infant child was also frequently flogged by Mrs. Gatewood, for crying, until its skin was bruised literally purple. This kind of treatment was what drove me from home and family, to seek a better home for them. But I am willing to forget the past. I should be Pleased to hear from you again, on the reception of this, and should also be very happy to correspond with you often, if it should be agreeable to yourself. I subscribe myself a friend to the oppressed, and Liberty forever.*

* Henry Bibb, *Narrative of the Life and Adventures of Henry Bibb, an American Slave, Written by Himself*. New York: Published by the author, 1849, pp. 175–178. Available online. URL: http://docsouth.unc.edu/neh/bibb/menu.html.

(continued from page 29)

slave trade ended by law in 1808, the domestic slave trade grew. Slaves torn from their families were bought and sold at crowded markets and auctions in Baltimore, Richmond, New Orleans, Washington, D.C., and other cities and county seats. Kept in crowded pens like animals until the auction began, they were assessed for their health and ability to work. The worth of women depended on if they could bear children—more slaves for their owner. "The auction block and the brutal overseer became his dread while awake, his nightmare when asleep,"[5] Siebert writes. Buyers had little regard for whether a slave had a child or a husband from whom she would be separated forever. On March 3, 1859, the race course at Savannah, Georgia, was packed with people. They had come to one of the largest slave auctions in American history: 436 men, women, children, and babies were to be sold. The slaves were owned by Pierce M. Butler, a Philadelphia man who had inherited rice and cotton plantations in the South. Deeply in debt, he was selling the slaves to pay his creditors. This infamous sale has been called "the weeping time" because it tore apart so many families.

Most slaves who risked their lives to escape, however, were intent on ending the poverty, pain, and fear that they had endured in a life of captivity. Henry Bibb, a slave from Kentucky, experienced a childhood marked by frequent beatings. Bibb writes in *Narrative of the Life and Adventures of Henry Bibb*:

> I was brought up in [Kentucky]. Or, more correctly speaking, ... I was flogged up; for where I should have received moral, mental, and religious instruction I received stripes without number, the object of which was to degrade and keep me in subordination.... I have been dragged down to the lowest depths of human degradation and wretchedness, by Slaveholders.[6]

Freedom, for Bibb and thousands of others, meant a life of safety and release from pain.

Not all owner-slave relationships were marked by cruelty. Slaves sometimes felt a certain loyalty to their owners. Many owners felt that they were benevolently caring for slaves and their families, offering them food, shelter, and protection, in a relationship that was morally right. But the institution of slavery could never be anything but what it was. Slavery was, in historian Deborah Gray White's words, a system of forced labor in which Africans were compelled to do the work that whites would not or could not be made to do. In other words, she writes, "White folks had all the power, and black folks survived."[7] Because of that essential imbalance, the desire for freedom was a powerful one.

SAFE HOUSES

Slaves traveling on the Underground Railroad would move from one hiding spot to another, though the stops and routes were not always planned ahead. Sometimes the direction that a fugitive took had to change at the last minute because of unforeseen dangers or obstacles. Often the slaves slept huddled under bushes or behind a barn out in the open, vulnerable to rain or snow or cold winter winds. If they were fortunate, they would stay in the houses or barns of freed slaves, white abolitionists, and other sympathizers.

The safe house might be Thomas Garrett's store in Wilmington, Delaware; Abigail and Elizabeth Goodwin's modest white house in Salem, New Jersey; the brick Plymouth Church of the Pilgrims in Brooklyn, New York; or a Quaker farm called Rokeby in the Champlain Valley of Vermont near the Canadian border. At a safe house, the runaways were given food, clothing, and money to tide them over. Then, if contacts could be made through messengers or a note taken secretly, the slaves would be sent on with directions to the next safe house—where someone else would be waiting for them.

Those involved in the Underground Railroad used railroad terms to communicate. The routes from safe house to safe house were called lines and were about 15 miles long. The farther north one got, the shorter the distance. Pictured is the Magee House in Canesto, New York, which was used as a safe house in 1855.

ROUTES TO FREEDOM

The worst dangers lay close to home, where a farmer or a shopkeeper might recognize the escaped slaves or their owners might see them. To avoid immediate capture, slaves took off in the blackness of night. Saturday night was a good night to leave, because Sunday was the slaves' day off and no one would miss them in the fields or at the owner's house. Sometimes they fled without a direction in mind. They hid on a nearby farm or just down the road. If they could make it farther, they sought the Atlantic coast or river valleys that they could follow north. Sometimes they simply ran into tracts of wilderness, where they hid as long as they could. "Drives to flush out runaways from forests and swamps were popular sporting events in some parts of the South,"[8] Bordewich writes.

The only sure direction to freedom was northward. Ever since Congress passed the Missouri Compromise in 1820, which allowed Maine to enter the Union as a free state and Missouri as a slave state, the line between slave and non-slave states had been dug deeper. Part of the Compromise was that slavery would not be allowed north of the southern border of Missouri, except in Missouri. Farther east, the famous Mason-Dixon Line—originally a surveyor's line drawn to solve a border dispute—divided the slave states of Maryland, Delaware, and Virginia (what is now West Virginia) from the free state of Pennsylvania. These lines were as real geographically as they were powerful symbolically. Like rivers, they had to be crossed to get to the other side of freedom.

Slaves in the Deep South fled to Florida and Louisiana when the areas were under Spanish rule and by boat to Caribbean islands. Slaves in Texas headed south across the Rio Grande to Mexico, which, like Canada, offered a permanent refuge. In truth, it was extremely difficult for slaves from Alabama, Georgia, and other states to reach Pennsylvania or New York, but some were able to do so. In December 1848, the slave couple Ellen and William Craft ran off from their owners in Georgia. Ellen, who was the daughter of a slave and her white owner, posed as a white man, and William pretended to be Ellen's slave. They traveled by stagecoach, train, and boat for 1,000 miles (1,609 kilometers) and arrived safely in Boston. Even then, their Georgia owner sent agents all the way to Boston to find them. Abolitionists had welcomed the Crafts and protected them, but the only sure freedom was out of the country. The couple fled to England, returning only after the Civil War. Others in the Deep South left plantations and wandered in the woods and roads, hungry and lost, and then returned to their owners. Some did not survive.

Most slaves who had successful journeys on the Underground Railroad were from the border states of Delaware, Maryland, Virginia, and Kentucky, where the distances to freedom were not as great and there were more freed blacks and abolitionists willing to offer aid. There were several main routes, but even those were not set in stone. In the interior, slaves coming up through Tennessee and Kentucky crossed the Ohio River to Ohio and Indiana and traveled north to the Great Lakes and Canada. From Maryland and Delaware, slaves crossed into Pennsylvania or New Jersey, then into New York State. They might travel up through Connecticut to abolitionist enclaves in Northampton or Boston and into northern New England, or take an inland route through northern New York State and over the Niagara River to Canada. Even within states, there were various routes along the way.

New Jersey had several tracks, but the state was not sympathetic to fugitive slaves and danger lurked everywhere. According to Siebert, the main route led from Philadelphia across the Delaware River to Camden. Fugitives were taken in by the Macedonia African Episcopal Church in Camden, run by its black pastor, Thomas Clement Oliver, a leader on the Underground Railroad. The runaway slaves then followed the Delaware River to Burlington City, where they could stay in the Burlington Pharmacy. They went on to Princeton and New Brunswick. The goal was to cross the Raritan River, but slave catchers patrolled the river. An Underground Railroad spy named Cornelius Cornell lived near the river, and he would signal when it was safe to cross. The slaves then headed to Jersey City along the Hudson River. Abolitionists there helped fugitives onto ferries across the Hudson to New York City. If they could get to Grand Central Station, they would board a train for Syracuse, New York, and then be free to move on to Canada.

Near the border to Canada, abolitionists and freed blacks offered important assistance for the last leg of the journey. In the Midwest, the city of Detroit, Michigan, was a popular place for fugitives to cross to Canada. A white hotel owner named Seymour Finney let slaves stay in his barn, and the Second Baptist Church opened its doors to fugitives, too. Others also helped harbor slaves until they could travel farther. George DeBaptiste, an African-American barber and businessman, had a ship called the *T. Whitney*, which he used to transport runaway slaves across the Detroit River to Windsor, Ontario.

ABOLITIONISTS

Around the time that Tice Davids crossed the Ohio River, the abolitionist movement was growing. Abolitionists wanted an immediate end to slavery and the emancipation of all slaves. On January 1, 1831, the Massachusetts abolitionist William Lloyd Garrison published the first issue of his weekly newspaper, *The Liberator*. Little did he know then that he would continue to publish the paper for more than 30 years until slavery was finally abolished in 1865. The number of subscribers was only around 400, and a majority of his readers were African American. Garrison filled the pages with news and opinion about slavery. In the paper's first issue, Garrison addressed a letter "To the Public," explaining why abolishing slavery was so urgent:

> I am aware, that many object to the severity of my language; but is there not cause for severity? I *will* be as harsh as truth, and as uncompromising as justice. On this subject, I do not wish to think, or speak, or write, with moderation. No! No! Tell a man whose house is on fire, to give a moderate alarm; tell him to moderately rescue his wife from the hand of the ravisher; tell the mother to gradually extricate her babe from the fire into which it has fallen;—but urge me not to use moderation in a cause like the present. I am in earnest—I will not equivocate—I will not excuse—I will not retreat a single inch—AND I WILL BE HEARD. The apathy of the people is enough to make every statue leap from its pedestal, and to hasten the resurrection of the dead.[9]

Garrison did not mind controversy. The son of Canadian immigrants, he was born in 1805 in Newburyport, Massachusetts. His father left, and the family struggled so Garrison went to work as an apprentice at a young age to a shoemaker. He started to work for a newspaper printer when he was just 13, gaining skills he would use as an abolitionist. Like others around him, as he entered adulthood, Garrison was swept up in a religious revival known as the Second Great Awakening. Lasting from the 1790s to the 1840s, this movement of heightened religious fervor and a spirit of evangelism included a new social activism. Preachers urged their flocks to create a better, and more moral, world by reforming prisons, avoiding alcohol, and abolishing slavery. Religious leaders preached about the outrage of slavery. In contrast to the earlier Puritans, who used religion to justify slavery, followers of the Second Great Awakening believed that slavery went against Christian beliefs. Garrison called slaveholding a crime.

Not wanting to join in politics but hoping to use his influence in other ways, Garrison and several other abolitionists founded the New England Anti-Slavery Society in Boston in 1832. "Whereas, we believe that Slavery is contrary to the precepts of Christianity, dangerous to the liberties of the country, and ought immediately to be abolished; and whereas, we believe that the citizens of New England not only have the right to protest against it, but are under the highest obligation to seek its removal by moral influence; and whereas we believe that the free people of color are unrighteously oppressed . . . we agree to form ourselves into a Society," the society's constitution stated.[10] In 1833, Garrison and others, including abolitionist brothers Lewis and Arthur Tappan, met in Philadelphia to found the American Anti-Slavery Society, one of the largest abolitionist organizations.

Antislavery organizations grew rapidly during the next years. The Vermont Anti-Slavery Society started in February 1835, followed by the New York Anti-Slavery Society. Local

Abolitionist William Lloyd Garrison promoted the immediate emancipation of slaves in his antislavery newspaper, *The Liberator* (1831–1865). The publication gained subscribers over the three decades of its existence until his "Valedictory" column in the final issue after the end of the Civil War.

societies formed throughout the Northern and Midwestern states, including Ohio, Indiana, and Illinois. In small towns across the country, people met to start local groups, publish pamphlets and newspapers, hold meetings, raise money, and provide assistance to runaway slaves. They also opened their homes for use as safe houses for fugitives, thus becoming part of the Underground Railroad.

A RADICAL IDEA

Garrison's call for immediate emancipation was a radical idea. Not all antislavery advocates were ready to support it. Some people did not favor slavery but also did not believe that blacks should have equal rights or become citizens. Others felt that blacks should return to Africa and resettle there. The American Colonization Society was formed in 1817 to send freed blacks back to Africa. In 1822, the society founded a colony on the west coast of Africa that became the country of Liberia in 1847. Abolitionists criticized this movement as racist and an excuse for slaveholders to continue slavery.

Still others proposed gradual abolition, with the idea that slavery would eventually disappear on its own without the need for new antislavery laws. Several states, including Connecticut, New Jersey, Rhode Island, and Pennsylvania, passed laws in the late 1700s to abolish slavery gradually, rather than ending it all at once. Slaves were given their freedom after a certain number of years. Sometimes their children would be given their freedom first. This resulted in much uncertainty for generations of slaves, many of whom waited a lifetime for freedom. Gradual emancipation was passed in New York in 1799. The law stated that a person born after July 4, 1799, had to spend only a certain number of years in slavery, depending on whether they were male or female. Then they would be emancipated. In 1827, slavery was finally abolished in New York.

Most abolitionists were not just opposed to slavery but wanted to fully include African Americans in society, with equal rights and citizenship. To many people at the time, this idea was nothing short of revolutionary and extremist.

Southern slave owners were incensed that abolitionists were turning upside down the order of their society. They believed that the abolitionists were lawbreakers, determined to destroy the national economy. Among many Northerners, opposition to abolitionists was also heated. Northern economies relied on slavery, too, through trade in goods and services.

In New York City, a center of commerce, people's views on slavery were mixed. While many did not favor slavery, the city's economy was tied up in the cotton industry. Cotton was shipped from Southern plantations to Manhattan's busy harbor and loaded on ships bound for England. Bankers and merchants in New York provided financing to Southern cotton businesses. State legislators often voted in favor of federal pro-slavery laws because of this reliance on the cotton trade. Yet in the late 1830s, a strong abolitionist movement was under way, led by Isaac T. Hopper, the Philadelphia Quaker, and David Ruggles, a printer and journalist who opened the first African-American bookstore in his small grocery store. Ruggles published pamphlets and magazines against slavery and led the New York Committee of Vigilance, which defended African Americans in court. The abolitionists faced plenty of opposition. On July 4, 1834, a riot erupted outside an abolitionist lecture at a chapel on Chatham Street. Ruggles's store was burned down.

Even in Philadelphia, a more tolerant city, opposition to abolitionists was sometimes violent. On May 17, 1838, a mob, angered by the words of the speakers, destroyed Philadelphia Hall, a meeting place for abolitionists and suffragettes who favored a woman's right to vote. On that night, Angelina Grimke, the daughter of a slave-owning judge in South Carolina, spoke out in favor of the emancipation of slaves. The angry mob set fire to the hall. In other cities, anti-abolition riots also took place. A hostile mob killed an abolitionist newspaper publisher in Alton, Illinois, named Elijah Lovejoy. An anti-abolitionist riot took place in Cincinnati.

NAT TURNER'S REBELLION

Violence occurred on both sides, but few incidents were as brazen as the one that became known as Nat Turner's Rebellion. Turner was a slave, born in 1800. He grew up on a large plantation in Southampton County, Virginia. He learned to read and write, which was unusual at the time. Turner was also very religious and believed that God sent him messages through spiritual visions and signs from nature. Other slaves called him "The Prophet" and listened to him preach at Baptist services. Turner believed that God had chosen him to lead the slaves to freedom.

He ran away in 1821 but returned after seeing a vision. After his owner died, he was sold and passed to several owners, while his visions grew stronger. Turner later recounted that on May 12, 1828, he heard a loud noise:

> [A]nd the Spirit instantly appeared to me and said the Serpent was loosened, and Christ had laid down the yoke he had borne for the sins of men, and that I should take it on and fight against the Serpent, for the time was fast approaching when the first should be last and the last should be first.... I should arise and prepare myself and slay my enemies with their own weapons.[11]

In February 1831, Turner witnessed an eclipse of the sun. He thought it was a black man's hand over the sun and a sign from God telling him to revolt against slavery. After another eclipse in early August, Turner prepared his rebellion. On August 21, Turner gathered six slaves, and they went on a rampage. They killed the family of Turner's master. Then with the help of a growing number of slaves, the group went on to kill 57 men, women, and children before the militia came after them. Some of the slaves were caught, but Turner eluded capture for several weeks. On October 31, a local farmer found him and turned him in to the authorities.

Turner was convicted of insurrection and sentenced to hang on November 11.

The rebellion ignited fear among whites in Virginia and elsewhere. Angry men began to kill slaves and chase freed and enslaved blacks out of Virginia. The Virginia General Assembly held a debate about slavery. Though some legislators believed that slavery should eventually be abolished, the consensus was that for now slavery was justified and slave rebellions had to be put down. The Virginia legislators passed more laws restricting slaves from preaching, gathering in groups, and being taught to read and write. "All African Americans, slave and free, were watched by patrols with their firearms ready. On a pole along the roadside the decapitated head of a slave was hoisted for all to see. It sent a message loud and clear. White power would not tolerate black resistance. Revolts for freedom were for white men only,"[12] historian Deborah Gray White writes. Nat Turner's Rebellion, and other revolts, helped set the stage for the Civil War and the end of slavery.

WILLIAM STILL AND HENRY "BOX" BROWN

Escaping on the Underground Railroad was its own form of rebellion. Slaves were defying the rules governing their lives, and abolitionists were tearing down the laws of society. Those who helped the fugitive slaves felt they had no choice. One abolitionist leader in Philadelphia was William Still. Born in 1821 in Burlington County, New Jersey, he was one of 17 or 18 children of an African-American couple. His father had bought his own freedom, while his mother had escaped from slavery, leaving two young sons behind to join her husband. Still grew up on their New Jersey farm. In 1844, he moved to Philadelphia, where he became a prosperous coal merchant, but he devoted much of his time to abolishing slavery and helping fugitive slaves. He served as president of the Pennsylvania Society for the Abolition of Slavery, and his home office was a major station on the Underground Railroad.

With the help of a sympathetic white storekeeper, Henry Brown devised a plan to have himself shipped in a dry goods box to a free state. Brown's box traveled by wagon (three times), railroad (three times), steamboat, and ferry on a 27-hour-long journey from Richmond, Virginia, to Philadelphia, Pennsylvania.

Still was often the first person that fugitives met when they arrived in Philadelphia. Along with providing them money, train tickets, and contacts for moving north or finding work and housing in Philadelphia, Still recorded their life stories and the tales of their escapes. Filling up many notebooks, which he kept hidden through the Civil War, Still patiently recorded small details, such as a runaway's height and hair color and the shoes they were given, or the person who helped them in Delaware. The stories later became a book, *The Underground Railroad*, published in 1872. Still's chronicles preserved the identities of hundreds of slaves, whose bravery would have been lost to history. He provided a first-person window into the Underground Railroad.

One of the most amazing stories was the escape of Henry Brown, a slave from Richmond, Virginia. In the spring of 1849, Brown wanted to run from his master but it was almost impossible to evade the slave catchers who roamed the city. So he devised an ingenious escape route—a box. As Still writes, "The size of the box and how it was to be made to fit him most comfortably, was of his own ordering. Two feet eight inches deep, two feet wide, and three feet long were the exact dimensions of the box, lined with baize [a type of fabric]. His resources in regard to food and water consisted of the following: One bladder of water and a few small biscuits."[13] Brown nailed himself into the box, addressed to an acquaintance in Philadelphia.

Brown's box traveled by wagon, then railroad, steamboat, wagon again, railroad, ferry, railroad, and finally delivery wagon. Some 26 hours later, he arrived in Philadelphia and was taken out, soaking wet and shaken, but alive. He was known as Henry "Box" Brown for his amazing journey to freedom. Newspaper reporters took his photograph and told his tale. Brown was famous, but not as well known as another of Still's friends, whose story he also wrote down. The same year that Brown traveled to freedom, a farmhand from Maryland took a very different journey. Like Brown, she met Still in Philadelphia after she arrived, weary from walking. Her name was Harriet Tubman.

4

Journey of Mercy

On a cold night in the winter of 1860, a woman waded determinedly through an icy swamp in Maryland. Harriet Tubman was short and sturdy, close to the ground and aware of the natural signals that might mean danger or a wrong turn. She listened for the broken branch, the breathing of dogs, the stone turned on a nearby road. Having grown up on farms and worked for years in the fields, she knew what sounds were part of the night woods and what sounds meant danger.

Behind her in the darkness were Stephen and Maria Ennals and their three children: Harriet, 6, Amanda, 4, and a 3-month-old baby. A man named John and another woman were also in the party. The group followed in Tubman's foot-steps, trying not to fall into freezing water. No one spoke aloud, fearing that slave catchers were in the woods and along nearby roads, waiting for them to make a mistake.

In 1849, Harriet Tubman escaped slavery, then returned to the slave state of Maryland to help others run away. With the help of antislavery activists and using safe houses on the Underground Railroad, Tubman made 13 missions and helped more than 70 slaves escape.

The baby, so small that it fit in a basket, was given medicine to sleep. A sudden cry could mean capture for all of them. Behind the travelers lay lives of slavery, with few hopes and no possibilities. Ahead of them lay the unknown, but the promise of freedom.

They had a long way to go. The Fugitive Slave Act of 1850, a stricter version of the act of 1793, had made nearby Pennsylvania a hazardous zone for runaway slaves. In fact, agents sent by their owners and federal marshals could catch fugitive slaves on any street in the country and send them back to their owners without a trial. Fortunately, Tubman would have help along the way. On this, her last trip on the Underground Railroad, she led her group to the station master Thomas Garrett in Wilmington, Delaware, who gave her money to hire a carriage. They rode on to Chester County, Pennsylvania, and from there to Philadelphia. Four weeks later, a few days before Christmas, they arrived in the safety of the upstate town of Auburn, New York. But first, on this dark night, each step forward meant both a step toward freedom and new dangers.

A GIRL NAMED MINTY ROSS

By then she was famous, known as "The Moses of Her People," after the biblical prophet who had led the Israelite slaves out of Egypt to freedom, but Harriet Tubman's life began with little fanfare and not much hope. She was born Araminta "Minty" Ross in Dorchester County, Maryland, a low-lying fertile land of wheat and corn fields, oak, hickory, and pine forests, slow-moving rivers, and pastures near Chesapeake Bay. The year she was born is not certain since slaves' births were not officially recorded, but it was around 1822.

Her parents, Harriet "Rit" Green and Ben Ross, were slaves. Rit was a house slave, owned by Mary Pattison Brodess. Ben worked on the timber plantation of his owner Anthony Thompson, who married Brodess after her first husband died. Rit and Ben's marriage was likely not official. Like many slave couples, they often lived apart as they got passed down through their owners' families. Minty was the fifth of nine children (four boys and five girls) born to the couple. After Mary Brodess died,

Rit and her children, including Minty, became the property of her son Edward Brodess, and they had to move to his house.

A BRIEF CHILDHOOD

Minty's childhood did not last long. Brodess was hard-pressed for money, so he used his young slaves to earn extra income. By the time she was five or six, Minty was sent out to work. One job was at the home of a woman named Miss Susan, who used a whip when she was not satisfied with the young girl's care of her baby or her household chores. Tubman later told her biographer Sarah H. Bradford about the experience:

> 'What do you mean by doing my work this way, you—!' and passing her finger on the table and piano, she showed her the mark it made through the dust. 'Miss Susan, I done sweep and dust just as you told me.' But the whip was already taken down, and the strokes were falling on head and face and neck. Four times this scene was repeated before breakfast."[1]

Miss Susan's sister, Emily, intervened when she could and helped Minty learn to do her tasks.

Through her early years, Minty would often be rented to other families, giving most of the money she earned to Brodess. As she grew older, she became a field hand. She worked outside from dawn to dusk, driving oxen, plowing, and lifting heavy loads. "I grew up like a neglected weed—ignorant of liberty, having no experience of it. Then I was not happy or contented; every time I saw a white man I was afraid of being carried away,"[2] she later told Benjamin Drew, an abolitionist who collected the stories of slaves in *A North-Side View of Slavery*. She had no education and never learned to read or write. Many slave states had laws forbidding the education of slaves, with steep fines for those who dared to do so.

A traumatic accident would leave lasting effects on the girl. One day, when she was a teenager, Minty was at a local store when another young slave tried to run off. His owner threw an iron weight at him, and Minty was in the way. She was hit on her head and almost died. Her mother, Rit, nursed her back to health, but the recovery took a long time. For the rest of her life, she would suffer from blackouts and sudden sleepiness, a serious condition that was probably epilepsy. After the accident, she was sent back to work.

Like most slaves, she had been raised in a religious Christian family, yet Minty grew even more spiritual as she healed from the trauma. "Appears like, I prayed all the time ... about my work, everywhere; I was always talking to the Lord. When I went to the horse-trough to wash my face, and took up the water in my hands, I said, 'Oh, Lord, wash me, make me clean.' When I took up the towel to wipe my face and hands, I cried, 'Oh, Lord, for Jesus' sake, wipe away all my sins!'"[3] she told Bradford. Religion would be a source of strength for Tubman as she endured continuing hardship and was forced time and time again to find immense courage.

ESCAPE

In 1844, Minty married a free black man named John Tubman and took his last name. At some point, she also changed her first name to Harriet, like her mother's. Tubman continued to work as she had for most of her life. She was hired out to Dr. Anthony C. Thompson, the son of her father's owner, who lived on the Choptank River in Poplar Neck in Caroline County, Maryland. She even earned enough money to buy a pair of oxen. In 1849, after her owner, Edward Brodess, died suddenly, she feared being sold south to settle the family debt. She was uneasy because her family had already been torn apart by the slave trade. In all, three of her sisters—Linah, Mariah Ritty, and Soph—had been sold away and never seen again.

For a slave to be sold through the domestic slave trade was a terrible fate. Separated from their children, spouses, brothers, sisters, and parents, possibly to endure life with a worse owner, slaves dreaded the prospect. That they might be sold farther south was also a fear. A slave's life on large cotton and rice plantations in Georgia or Mississippi was often more grueling than on the small farms and in industries farther north. Escape was also more difficult, and abolitionists in the border states and the North did not risk going far south to get a slave out. "While many sympathized with the slave in his chains, and freely wept over his destiny, or gave money to help buy his freedom, but few could be found who were willing to take the risk of going into the South, and standing face to face with Slavery, in order to conduct a panting slave to freedom, the undertaking was too fearful to think of in most cases,"[4] William Still, the Philadelphia abolitionist, wrote in his book on the Underground Railroad.

Thus, Tubman knew this might be her last chance to run for freedom. "For I had reasoned this out in my mind, there was one of two things I had a right to, liberty or death; if I could not have one, I would have the other,"[5] she later said. Her husband was already free so he would stay behind. She left with her two brothers, Ben and Henry, but after they decided to turn back, she was determined to go by herself. She had to keep her plans secret. Yet she later said that she sang a song to let people know she was going: "I'll meet you in the morning,/Safe in the promised land,/On the other side of Jordan,/Bound for the promised land."[6] One night in the late fall of 1849, Minty walked away from the slave quarters on Thompson's property. She started off on foot, hiding during the day and traveling after dark.

All she knew was to go north. "And so without money, and without friends, she started on through unknown regions; walking by night, hiding by day, but always conscious of an invisible pillar of cloud by day, and of fire by night, under the guidance of which she journeyed or rested,"[7] Bradford writes. Tubman likely had help from the Underground Railroad. A white woman may have given her a map. Tubman may have stopped at a safe house where she swept the yard for the woman, waiting until the husband arrived to hide her in his wagon and take her farther north, as Kate Clifford Larson relates in her Tubman biography, *Bound for the Promised Land.* Others may have also helped her along the way.

When she had stepped over the border into Pennsylvania, Tubman felt full of joy and promise, as she later recalled. "When I found I had crossed that line, . . . I looked at my hands to see if I was the same person. There was such a glory over everything; the sun came like gold through the trees, and over the fields, and I felt like I was in Heaven."[8] Her destination was Philadelphia, a city that had seen slave ships unload at its docks, but now had a large free black population. A law for the gradual emancipation of slaves was passed in Pennsylvania in 1780. By the time Tubman arrived there, Philadelphia offered opportunity for a freed slave needing work and housing.

FREEDOM

Having lived her life in rural Maryland, Philadelphia was an unfamiliar new world for Tubman. She met leading abolitionists like Lydia Maria Child and William Still and learned more about what was going on in the world. Tubman worked as a cook and a maid in Philadelphia and Cape May, New Jersey, but she was lonely and missed her family. She was determined to bring them to freedom, too. In December 1850, Tubman did the unthinkable. She walked back into the slave state of Maryland, risking capture and punishment, to help her family escape.

The first people she saved were her niece Kessiah Jolley Bowley and Bowley's two children. They had been taken to the auction block to be sold, but with the help of Kessiah's husband Tubman was able to lead them away. She took them through Baltimore and on to Philadelphia. Her next trip was to rescue her brother Moses and two other men. Over the next 10 years, Tubman traveled back to Maryland 13 times, bringing most of her family to freedom, including three other brothers, Robert, Ben, and Henry, as well as her parents, according to Larson.

This painting depicts Harriet Tubman leading escaped slaves into Canada. Tubman usually traveled in the winter because of the long, dark nights. She also carried a gun and started the journey on Saturdays because slaves had the day off on Sundays and masters would not notice they were gone until Mondays. She was said to have "never lost a passenger."

Tubman became one of the most famous "conductors" on the Underground Railroad, known for never losing a passenger.

SLAVE STEALING

Tubman did not work alone. She had the help of many, including two people who were especially important, not just to Tubman but to hundreds of other fugitives—William Still and Thomas Garrett. "Harriet seems to have a special angel to guard her on her journey of mercy,"[9] wrote Garrett, the Wilmington station master who was a friend to Tubman. One of her angels was Garrett himself.

Garrett had paid a high price for helping on the Underground Railroad. In 1848, Garrett and another abolitionist, John Hunn, were caught assisting a slave family to escape to Pennsylvania. They were tried before the federal court at the New Castle Court House (in Delaware) for violating the Fugitive Slave Act of 1793. Found guilty, Garrett was fined $5,400 and went bankrupt. Nevertheless, in the courtroom, he spoke out in defiance. "Thou has left me without a dollar. . . . I say to thee and to all in this courtroom, that if anyone knows a fugitive who wants shelter . . . send him to Thomas Garrett and he will befriend him."[10] Through the 1850s, Garrett helped Tubman every time she passed through Wilmington, Delaware, leading fugitive slaves from Maryland to Philadelphia. He gave her money, supplies, and safe hiding, and made sure she had a place to stay the next night on her journey. In 1860, Garrett was still working on the Underground Railroad when the Maryland legislature offered a $10,000 reward for anyone who could arrest him for slave stealing.

Tubman, too, had unusual determination. One night, she was leading a passenger who wanted to turn back. If he gave up, he could have put the whole group in jeopardy. Tubman raised a gun to him, persuading him to change his mind and keep going.

THE NORTH STAR

In Maryland and other border states, slave catchers were likely to be out on the back roads and by the fields, on the lookout for runaway slaves. Often they had hound dogs that could track the smell of people. Most communities in the South hired patrollers who watched the slaves and punished those who gathered in groups or left their plantation. Some were professional bounty hunters, who tracked down runaways for a living. After capture, the punishment was often flogging. But the patrollers and slave catchers were also allowed to shoot blacks who did not surrender. Often they were not motivated by following the law but by the money they received for catching a slave.

To elude the slave catchers, Tubman would travel in the small rivers, streams, and swamps that wound through farms and woodlands in Maryland. The waterways were like train tracks for Tubman and other fugitives. Wading in the water helped to throw off their scents and confuse the hound dogs. Disguises also helped. On one of her trips back, she came perilously close to being seen by her owner. As Bradford recounts:

> With a daring almost heedless, she went even to the very village where she would be most likely to meet one of the masters to whom she had been hired; and having stopped at the market and bought a pair of live fowls, she went along the street with her sun-bonnet well over her face, and with the bent and decrepit air of an aged woman. Suddenly on turning a corner, she spied her old master coming towards her. She pulled the string which tied the legs of the chickens; they began to flutter and scream, and as her master passed, she was stooping and busily engaged in attending to the fluttering fowls. And he went on his way, little thinking that he was brushing the very garments of the woman who had dared to steal herself, and others of his belongings.[11]

With no official maps, compasses, or highway signs to lead them through the fields, swamps, and woods, Tubman and other fugitive slaves relied on natural landmarks to show them the way. One of the most certain beacons was the North Star, long used by travelers around the globe as a navigational tool on land and sea. The North Star is part of the Little Dipper, a group of bright stars in the constellation Ursa Minor, or Little

Bear. It is easy for anyone to locate them on a clear night. Four stars form the bowl and three stars form the handle. The last star on the handle is Polaris (Pole Star), or the North Star, which points to the North Pole.

By following the bright star, slaves could be sure that they were heading north, though they might not know their exact location. The star also became a symbol of freedom. When Frederick Douglass started his antislavery newspaper in 1847 in Rochester, New York, he called it *The North Star*. The motto of the newspaper was: "Right is of no Sex—Truth is of no Color—God is the Father of us all, and we are all brethren."[12]

"GO DOWN, MOSES"

Music was an important part of the lives of slaves, particularly spirituals, the religious folk songs. Spirituals were rooted in the traditional rhythms and melodies of the music of West Africa, where the slaves and their ancestors had come from. Slaves sang to express their feelings, religious beliefs, and deep desire for release from their harsh lives. "Oh go down, Moses, Way down in Egypt land/Tell old Pharaoh/Let my people go,"[13] rang the words of the famous spiritual "Go Down, Moses." As more slaves tried to flee to freedom in the nineteenth century, the songs may have helped inspire them. Many times, the lyrics described the journey to freedom. Frederick Douglass wrote that the lyrics "I thought I heard them say./There were lions in the way./I don't expect to stay/Much longer here"[14] were not about slaves meeting in heaven, but rather it was about runaway slaves reaching freedom in the North. "In the lips of some, it meant the expectation of a speedy summons to a world of spirits; but, in the lips of *our* company, it simply meant, a speedy pilgrimage toward a free state, and deliverance from all the evils and dangers of slavery,"[15] he wrote.

Historians are not certain how spirituals might have been used to communicate on the Underground Railroad, or whether the songs actually had coded or secret messages. Song lyrics can be interpreted in different ways. The well-known spiritual "Chariot's A'Coming" may have announced the arrival of a conductor, preparing to help slaves escape, for example. Or the song may have had a religious message about death and heaven. Other songs had lyrics that could be interpreted as maps, directing fugitives on their path northward.

Yet spirituals were popular and familiar to slaves and freed blacks, and they were sung on many occasions for various reasons. The songs were full of the spirit possessed by Tubman and other slaves seeking freedom—the spirit to resist captivity, seek freedom, declare solidarity and community, and keep hope alive. "They were tones, loud, long and deep, breathing the prayer and complaint of souls boiling over with the bitterest anguish. Every tone was testimony against slavery, and a prayer to God for deliverance from chains,"[16] Douglass wrote. Harriet Tubman was said to have had a beautiful singing voice.

CANADA

Tubman went back to Maryland in December 1854, arriving on Christmas Day to bring her brothers to Philadelphia. She led them to St. Catharines, Ontario, a refuge for fugitive slaves. In the next years, she made more trips to Maryland's Eastern Shore. She rescued her sister Rachel, Rachel's children, and several other friends and relatives who also settled in Canada. In the spring of 1857, Tubman made one of her most difficult rescues, leading her elderly parents out of Maryland. Her father was already free, but her mother was not. Her father was also in danger of being caught for helping fugitive slaves. The journey was treacherous, especially because of their ages. To get them out of Caroline County, where they were living, Tubman hobbled together a buggy from spare parts and bought a horse. She drove her parents to Thomas Garrett in Wilmington, who arranged for their passage to Ontario to join her brothers. Tubman also spent time in St. Catharines and had a house there.

For fugitive slaves, Canada was truly Canaan, or the Promised Land. In 1793, the then-British colony ended the importation of slaves and required that children born to enslaved women be set free at the age of 25. Their children were to be free at birth. By 1820, Canada stopped allowing fugitive slaves to be captured and taken back to the United States. Instead, Canada supported the migration of fugitive slaves into existing communities and new settlements.

JOSIAH HENSON

Josiah Henson was born a slave in Charles County, Maryland, in 1789. Before he was 18, he had been sold three times. He saved $350 to buy his freedom, but when he gave it to his owner he was told the price had gone up. Freedom would now cost him $1,000. Unwilling to put up with anymore, Henson ran off with his wife and four children. With assistance from the Underground Railroad and kind strangers, the family made it to Canada. There he became a Methodist minister and founded the Dawn Settlement near Dresden, Ontario, a community for escaped slaves, with farms, a sawmill, a gristmill, a brickyard, and a vocational school. Henson may have been the inspiration for the main character in *Uncle Tom's Cabin* by Harriet Beecher Stowe, who had read his autobiography. In this excerpt from *Truth Stranger than Fiction: Father Henson's Story of His Own Life* (1858), Henson describes his family being sold at a slave auction after their owner has died:

My brothers and sisters were bid off first, and one by one, while my mother, paralyzed by grief, held me by the hand. Her turn came, and she was bought by Isaac Riley of Montgomery County.

Fugitive slaves crossed the Canadian border from many locations. Some were able to cross the St. Lawrence River from New York. Some took boats across Lake Champlain. Others crossed the Detroit River to Ontario. The busiest region for crossings was between Oswego, New York, on Lake Ontario and Detroit, Michigan, on the Detroit River near Lake Erie. While they tried to get passages on ferries and other river and lake boats, some runaways walked over the winter ice on the

Then I was offered to the assembled purchasers. My mother, half distracted with the thought of parting forever from all her children, pushed through the crowd, while the bidding for me was going on, to the spot where Riley was standing. She fell at his feet and clung to his knees, entreating him in tones that a mother only could command, to buy her baby as well as herself, and spare to her one, at least, of her little ones. Will it, can it be believed that this man, thus appealed to, was capable not merely of turning a deaf ear to her supplication, but of disengaging himself from her with such violent blows and kicks, as to reduce her to the necessity of creeping out of his reach, and mingling the groan of bodily suffering with the sob of a breaking heart? As she crawled away from the brutal man I heard her sob out, "Oh, Lord Jesus, how long, how long shall I suffer this way!" I must have been then between five and six years old. I seem to see and hear my poor weeping mother now. This was one of my earliest observations of men.*

*Josiah Henson, *Truth Stranger than Fiction: Father Henson's Story of His Own Life*. Boston: John P. Jewitt & Co., 1858, pp. 12–13. Available online. URL: http://docsouth.unc.edu/neh/henson58/henson58.html.

Niagara River and Lake Erie, according to Bordewich. Most runaways headed to the land that is now southern Ontario. Others went to Newfoundland. Before the Civil War, as many as 30,000 to 100,000 fugitive slaves may have settled in Canada, but the numbers are uncertain.

Blacks in Canada had the rights of citizenship and were allowed to serve on juries and vote. "Paradoxically, it was in Canada that blacks became real Americans. Only there were they completely free to pursue the American dream of personal liberty, the acquisition of property, self-improvement, and the unfettered pursuit of happiness,"[17] Bordewich writes. Indeed, when the Kentucky governor demanded that a fugitive, Jesse Happy, who had allegedly stolen his owner's horse, be returned to Kentucky, he received a letter from Canada's lieutenant governor, Francis Head, saying that "the slave owner is not only the aggressor, but the blackest criminal of the two—it is the case of the dealer in human flesh versus the stealer of horse flesh,"[18] Bordewich reports.

The fugitives arrived in Canada destitute and hungry but not alone. They joined other African-American families who fled with the British after the Revolutionary War. Fugitives settled in both towns and rural areas. Abolitionists even founded new settlements for escaped slaves, including the Refugees' Home Colony in Windsor, Ontario. Windsor lies just across the Detroit River from Detroit. Henry Bigg, the colony's founder, helped to establish schools, a church, and farms for the new settlers. He encouraged other runaway slaves and free blacks to move north and prosper.

Tubman's parents, along with her brothers, lived for several years in Ontario before Tubman resettled them in Auburn, New York, an upstate town that welcomed fugitive slaves. In her 13 trips back into Maryland, Tubman saved an estimated 70 people and helped countless others with advice and support. Frederick Douglass later celebrated Tubman for her courage. "The midnight sky and the silent stars have been the witnesses of your devotion to freedom and of your heroism. Excepting John Brown—of sacred memory—I know of no one who has willingly encountered more perils and hardships to serve our enslaved people than you have," Douglass wrote. "Much that you have done would seem improbable to those who do not know you as I know you. It is to me a great pleasure and a great privilege to bear testimony to your character and your works, and to say to those to whom you may come, that I regard you in every way truthful and trustworthy."[19]

A Law of Right

While the distance from Georgia or Alabama to the Mason-Dixon Line was too far for many fugitive slaves to travel successfully, slaves who lived in the border and mid-Atlantic states—like Virginia—had a better chance. Virginia's port cities had large populations of both freed and enslaved African Americans, many of whom were ready to help others to freedom. The slaves in these cities sometimes lived on their own and worked in local industries for a small wage, most of which they had to give to their owners who lived elsewhere. Surrounded by community activities such as churches, newspapers, and abolitionist organizations, the slaves in Norfolk and other Virginia cities were well informed about current politics and the antislavery movement. Some became conductors and agents on the Underground Railroad. They helped the fugitive journeys of local slaves as well as runaways from the Carolinas and other nearby states.

BY BOAT

Virginia was a well-worn pathway on the Underground Railroad, particularly for those traveling up the Atlantic seaboard by boat. The state's many rivers and inland waterways, along with its access to the Atlantic coast, offered numerous water escape routes. Fugitives left from the busy harbors of Norfolk, Portsmouth, Alexandria, and Richmond on boats bound for New York City, ports in Connecticut, Boston and New Bedford, Massachusetts, and even Nova Scotia. Sometimes they had to stow away or disguise themselves as freed slaves or servants, but a few captains were willing to take the fugitives for a price.

In his book *Underground Railroad*, Philadelphia abolitionist William Still recorded the journeys of many slaves by boat: Five slaves from Portsmouth, Virginia, were able to sail up the Atlantic and through the Delaware Bay. Four men from Lewes, Delaware, stole a boat and rowed through a storm to the South Jersey shore. The captain of an oyster schooner discovered them and helped them to get to Philadelphia. Susan Brooks, a slave from Norfolk, disguised herself as a laundress to board a ship bound for the North. She hid below the decks until the ship arrived at shore and she was free, Still reported. Despite the success stories, the journey by sea was one of the most treacherous ways to travel, and for many it did not end well.

Many escapees were captured, as in the case of the slaves hidden on the *Keziah*, a Delaware schooner that had stopped in Petersburg, Virginia. The river city of Petersburg was home to many former slaves, freed after the American Revolution. They had established a free black community on Pocahontas Island on the Appomattox River. Many were active in the Underground Railroad. In late May 1858, the *Keziah* left the harbor at Petersburg, and shortly after, five slaves were discovered missing from shore. A steamer was sent after the ship. When the slaves were brought back, the slave owners were so mad that they almost attacked them. The ship's captain was

William Baylis, a white agent for the Underground Railroad who had done this before. According to some reports, he charged for his services, and so made a living at helping fugitive slaves escape. Baylis was sentenced to 40 years in prison and served six years before Jefferson Davis pardoned him during the Civil War.

THE *PEARL*

One of the most daring attempts at escape by sea occurred in the spring of 1848 in Washington, D.C. The nation's capital was a crowded city of politicians, abolitionists, slave owners, slaves, and freed blacks. Washington held a major slave auction, and its inhumane slave pens held those waiting to be sold like cattle. The fact that the slave trade occurred within blocks of the White House and other federal buildings made slavery there even more controversial. While most Southern cities did not have much abolitionist activity, Washington was different.

In the spring of 1848, a freed slave named Daniel Bell was worried that his large family would be claimed back by the widow of the slave owner who had freed them. He asked William Chaplin, an abolitionist, to help the family escape. Chaplin sought funding from other abolitionists and contacted Daniel Drayton, a seaman who had helped a family of slaves escape by boat to Philadelphia. To assist the Bells, Drayton needed a boat. He asked Edward Sayers, the captain of a 54-ton schooner, the *Pearl*, if he could use his boat. He paid Sayers $100. Meanwhile, news of the planned escape drew the interest of slaves from Washington, Georgetown, and Alexandria, many of whom were owned by leading citizens. A freed slave named Paul Jennings, once owned by former President James Madison, helped organize the escape.

In the midst of city celebrations of the recent French Revolution on April 15, dozens of slaves sneaked from their quarters in the dark of night and went down to the Potomac River where the *Pearl* was docked. The fugitives included two

A Slave-Coffle passing the Capitol.

According to some historians, of the 600 or so people who worked to build the Capitol and the White House, about 400 were slaves. On the site where the Supreme Court sits today, the slave market was so strong that slave owners had to rent public jail space in order to hold the slaves. In this painting, slaves walk past the unfinished Capitol building in Washington, D.C., before the Civil War.

girls, Mary and Emily Edmondson, and their four brothers. The organizers had no idea that so many slaves would show up—some 70 or more men, women, and children. As the boat headed down the Potomac for the Chesapeake Bay, the tides and the winds turned against it. The boat became stuck at the mouth of the bay and could not move. News of the escape spread quickly when the slaves' owners awoke the next morning to find their property gone. Men on a steamboat came out looking for the fugitives.

The slaves were quickly recaptured and marched through the city to jail. Later, most were sold south because their owners wanted to get rid of them. The sisters Mary and Emily narrowly escaped that fate. They were members of the Methodist church, and Methodists in the North sent money to buy their freedom. The *Pearl* incident angered local slave owners and led to several days of rioting in the streets. Abolitionists were outraged, too, and called for the end of the slave trade in Washington, D.C. Two of the white men who piloted the *Pearl* were tried and convicted. Escape attempts like this one made it easier for Congress, in 1850, to pass its landmark law against fugitive slaves.

A NEW LAW

In October 1850, slave catchers captured a fugitive slave from Maryland named James Hamlet on a street in New York City. After escaping from his owner, he had been living for several years as a free man and working as a porter in a store on Water Street. Like many slaves who had reached a free state, Hamlet had made a new life for himself. But the previous month, Congress had passed a federal law that made it easier for owners to capture runaway slaves. Mary Brown, his owner back in Baltimore, had ordered his recapture, and the new law made sure that he had few legal recourses, or rights, even though slavery had been outlawed for more than two decades in New York State. The black community in the city was not going to stand still. For the first time, they held rallies in City Hall Park and met at a local church. They were outraged that their freedom had become even more jeopardized. They raised $800 to buy Hamlet's freedom.

In Boston, a similar chain of events played out for Shadrach Minkins, a slave who had run away from Norfolk, Virginia, and was working as a waiter. On February 15, 1851, two federal agents pretending to be customers arrested him while he was working at a local coffeehouse. Minkins was taken to a courthouse for a hearing. Abolitionist lawyers volunteered to defend him. In the midst of the hearing, members of the Boston Vigilance Committee mobbed the courtroom and pulled Minkins away from the court officers. They were able to get him to Canada on the Underground Railroad. Nine abolitionists were indicted, including the black abolitionist leader Lewis Hayden, but all of them were acquitted.

Minkins and Hamlet were among the first victims of the new Fugitive Slave Act of 1850, but there would be many more. The controversial law that cracked down on runaway slaves in non-slave states deepened the divide between those who favored slavery and those who detested it, pushing the nation closer to civil war. Leading up to this legislation was a long, bitter feud between the South and the North over laws regarding fugitive slaves. The Fugitive Slave Act of 1793, which reinforced the fugitive slave clause in the Constitution, had not been effective. Many Northern states had ignored it, instead passing personal liberty laws that allowed local officials to refuse to arrest and return fugitives.

In 1842, the U.S. Supreme Court in the case of *Prigg v. Pennsylvania* took up the question of whether a professional slave catcher from Maryland could seize a runaway slave in Pennsylvania, which had a personal liberty law protecting fugitives, and return her to Maryland. The court decided that the state law was unconstitutional because it went against the federal law, but also that states did not have to carry out the federal law; it was up to the federal government to enforce it. Northern states continued to shield fugitives, even passing new laws forbidding officials from enforcing fugitive slave laws or holding runaways in jail.

By 1850, people in the slave states were alarmed, both by the numbers of runaway slaves and by the abolitionist movement to end slavery. More slaves were being lost to the Underground Railroad, and they feared that new territories and states admitted to the Union might ban slavery. Since the Missouri Compromise in 1820, the number of slave states and free states had been equal, but that balance was precarious. A crisis arose when California, buoyed by an influx of settlers with the Gold Rush, asked to enter the Union as a free state.

"THE MEANING OF JULY FOURTH FOR THE NEGRO"

During the 1850s, Frederick Douglass was a popular speaker on the abolitionist lecture circuit. He spent half the year traveling around the country, speaking out against slavery. His hometown of Rochester, New York, was a center of abolitionist activity, and he also attended events near home. On July 5, 1852, Frederick Douglass was invited to speak at a Fourth of July celebration at Corinthian Hall in Rochester. Among the speeches honoring the signing of the Declaration of Independence, Douglass's stood out for its oratory and anger. Like most of his lectures, Douglass's words that day were full of contempt for a government and nation that allowed slavery to continue. He refused to celebrate the day; instead, he said, he would be in mourning. Douglass urged blacks to unite for the painful struggle to win their liberty, and warned: "We must do this by labor, by suffering, by sacrifice, and if needs be, by our lives and the lives of others." Here is an excerpt from his famous speech:

> The rich inheritance of justice, liberty, prosperity and independence, bequeathed by your fathers, is shared by you, not by me. The sunlight that brought light and healing to you, has brought stripes and death to me. This Fourth of July is yours, not

Settlers on land ceded to the United States by Mexico after the Mexican-American War in 1848, an area encompassing present-day Arizona, New Mexico, Utah, Nevada, and parts of Colorado and Wyoming, were also seeking entrance into the Union. The question before Congress in the late summer of 1850 was whether the new states and territories would allow slavery or not.

mine. . . . Fellow-citizens, above your national, tumultuous joy, I hear the mournful wail of millions! Whose chains, heavy and grievous yesterday, are, today, rendered more intolerable by the jubilee shouts that reach them. . . .

What, to the American slave, is your Fourth of July? I answer; a day that reveals to him, more than all other days in the year, the gross injustice and cruelty to which he is the constant victim. To him, your celebration is a sham; your boasted liberty, an unholy license; your national greatness, swelling vanity; your sounds of rejoicing are empty and heartless; your denunciation of tyrants, brass-fronted impudence; your shouts of liberty and equality, hollow mockery; your prayers and hymns, your sermons and thanksgivings, with all your religious parade and solemnity, are, to him, mere bombast, fraud, deception, impiety, and hypocrisy—a thin veil to cover up crimes which would disgrace a nation of savages. There is not a nation on the earth guilty of practices more shocking and bloody than are the people of the United States, at this very hour.*

*Frederick Douglass, *My Bondage and My Freedom*. New York and Auburn: Miller, Orton & Mulligan, 1885, pp. 441–445. Available online. URL: http://docsouth.unc.edu/neh/douglass55/douglass55.html.

As he had in 1820, Congressman Henry Clay of Kentucky pushed for a compromise through a series of laws that would give something to both sides. He urged legislators to consider the importance of keeping the nation intact rather than focusing on their own states' interests. For seven months, the Senate hotly debated the issue, finally agreeing to the Compromise of 1850. The five laws allowed California to join the Union as a free state, tipping the balance in favor of free states. A new boundary was set between Texas and Mexico. The new territories of New Mexico and Utah could decide their slave status for themselves, while the slave trade in the District of Columbia was prohibited, though slavery was allowed to continue. In return for the changes that favored non-slave states, the Fugitive Slave Act was amended to satisfy the Southern bloc. For the first time, the government would be required to actively participate in returning fugitive slaves to their owners.

While the earlier federal law had given slave owners the right to reclaim their runaway slaves, now the government was obligated to help them do so. U.S. marshals had to chase fugitives and try to capture and return them or risk a $1,000 fine. Anyone caught assisting runaway slaves would be severely punished. Alleged fugitives had no right to a trial or even to present evidence before a federal commissioner.

RIOTS

This new law pleased the slave states, and slave owners hoped that it would stem the tide of runaways. Senator Jefferson Davis of Mississippi said during the debates on the law:

> Negroes do escape from Mississippi frequently . . . and the boats constantly passing by our long line of river frontier furnish great facility to get into Ohio; and when they do escape it is with great difficulty that they are recovered; indeed, it seldom occurs that they are restored. . . . We desire

laws that shall be effective . . . and be secured by penalties the most stringent which can be imposed.[1]

His comments echoed those of his Southern colleagues, who saw slaves fleeing their owners as causing huge financial losses for the Southern economy. Yet antislavery legislators were incensed that they would have to support slavery, and many were determined to defy the new law. "The freemen of Ohio will never turn out to chase the panting fugitive. They will never be metamorphosed into bloodhounds, to track him to his hiding place, and seize and drag him out, and deliver him to his tormentors," said Joshua R. Giddings, an antislavery congressman from Ohio. "We feel there is a law of right, of justice, of freedom, implanted in the breast of every intelligent human being, that bids him look with scorn upon this libel on all that is called law."[2] The opponents of the new law cited passages from the Bible that cautioned against helping to capture freed slaves, including this from Deuteronomy, 23:15: "Thou shalt *not* deliver unto his master the servant which is escaped from his master unto thee."[3]

The Fugitive Slave Act opened the gates to an ugly era of slave hunting. "Slave owners and their agents entered vigorously upon the chase, and a larger number of communities in the free states than ever before were invaded by men engaged in the disgusting business of capturing blacks," Wilbur Siebert writes in *The Underground Railroad*. Slaveholders hired slave catchers to retrieve their property. "He follows a negro with his dogs 36 hours after he has passed and never fails to overtake him. It is his profession and he makes some $600 annum at it."[4] Federal officers were also dispatched to find and retrieve fugitive slaves.

Those most affected included people like Hamlet, who had experienced freedom and now lived in constant fear of capture. Even free blacks who had never been enslaved were at risk of being caught, with no legal recourse. But even those fleeing slaves who could no longer find a safe haven in the free North did not have to despair. Instead, the Fugitive Slave Act sparked a new determination among abolitionists and those who worked on the Underground Railroad to put an end to slavery. In a fiery speech on July 5, 1852, Frederick Douglass said:

> In glaring violation of justice, in shameless disregard of the forms of administering law, in cunning arrangement to entrap the defenseless, and in diabolical intent, this fugitive slave law stands alone in the annals of tyrannical legislation.... I take this law to be one of the grossest infringements of Christian Liberty, and, if the churches and ministers of our country were not stupidly blind, or most wickedly indifferent, they, too, would so regard it.[5]

THE CASE OF ANTHONY BURNS

Abolitionists were willing to risk anything, even violence, to defy the law. In 1853, a slave named Anthony Burns escaped by boat from Richmond, Virginia. He arrived in Boston and got a job in a store on Brattle Street. On May 24, 1854, however, Burns was arrested under the Fugitive Slave Act. Abolitionists tried to free him without success, while U.S. president Franklin Pierce stepped into the fray, determined to show that the federal government was serious about enforcing the new law. At Burns's trial, abolitionists mobbed the courthouse and tried to set him free. A deputy federal marshal was stabbed and killed, and Burns remained in captivity.

The intense passions flared even higher, as federal troops and abolitionists continued to battle in the streets of Boston. Burns lost his trial and was put back on a boat to Virginia; his owner later sold him. Eventually, antislavery activists were able to buy Burns's freedom. Burns attended Oberlin College in Ohio, moved to Canada, and became a minister. This incident only drew more Bostonians and New Englanders to the side of the abolitionists.

The Fugitive Slave Act of 1850 was a major setback for abolitionists and fugitive slaves, including Anthony Burns. His arrest in Boston and subsequent return to his master in Virginia in 1854 turned many passive New Englanders against slavery. In this image Burns is surrounded by scenes of his capture, arrest, return to slavery, and his final days as pastor of a Baptist church in Canada.

In other states, similar revolts broke out against the Fugitive Slave Act. In Oberlin, Ohio, a federal marshal captured a fugitive slave named John Price in September 1858 and tried to take him back south. Hundreds of black and white abolitionists flocked to nearby Wellington, where Price was to board a train with federal authorities. The abolitionists helped Price to escape. First, he hid at Oberlin College, and then he was taken north to Canada. Thirty-seven people, including several Oberlin students, were arrested for violating the Fugitive Slave Act; only a white man, Simeon Bushnell, and a black man, Charles Langston, the grandfather of poet Langston Hughes, were convicted and went to jail. They appealed the case to the Ohio Supreme Court, which upheld the federal law. More than 10,000 people flocked to Cleveland to rally against the court's decision.

"ABOLITION GOLD"

The punishment for working on the Underground Railroad was severe. If caught, people could be made to pay steep fines or be thrown in jail for many years. Aiding fugitive slaves was considered a crime as bad as murder. Blacks who were caught providing assistance could be sent back into slavery. Samuel Burris was one of many black conductors on the Underground Railroad. Born a free man in Delaware, he lived in Philadelphia with his family but could not forget the slaves still in bondage in Maryland and Delaware. He began to travel back and forth to Maryland, helping to lead slaves back to Pennsylvania. Traveling into a slave state was treacherous for a black man, even if he was free. He could be captured and sold by unscrupulous slave catchers and traders. Unfortunately, that is just what happened. In June 1847, as he was smuggling a woman through Delaware, Burris was caught and jailed. He was put on trial and sentenced to be auctioned as a slave.

The Pennsylvania Anti-Slavery Society rallied behind Burris. An abolitionist named Isaac A. Flint was sent with money to the slave auction where Burris was to be sold.

William Still later chronicled the auction in his book on the Underground Railroad. "The usual opportunity was given to traders and speculators to thoroughly examine the property on the block, and most skillfully was Burris examined from the soles of his feet to the crown of his head; legs, arms and body, being handled as horse-jockeys treat horses," Still writes. Fortunately Flint was able to buy Burris with "abolition gold, to save him from going south," Still adds. "Once again Burris found himself in Philadelphia with his wife and children and friends, a stronger opponent than ever of slavery."[6] Never again did Burris venture into a slave state. He eventually moved to California, but still contributed money to help freed slaves.

KANSAS-NEBRASKA ACT OF 1854

The debate over slavery only grew more intense. Congress was again confronted with the issue when the transcontinental railroad was ready to push west into present-day Kansas and Nebraska. Legislators prepared to vote on admitting the two new territories, but first they had to decide about slavery. Northerners wanted slavery banned in the new territories, while Southern legislators did not. Senator Stephen A. Douglas of Illinois, chairman of the Senate Committee on Territories, advocated what he thought was a compromise, known as the Kansas-Nebraska Act of 1854. The law allowed popular sovereignty in the new territories. In other words, settlers would be allowed to vote whether to permit slavery or to prohibit it. Northerners and abolitionists were unhappy at this outcome. They felt it would allow the South to pressure the new territories to accept slavery. An Illinois lawyer and former congressman named Abraham Lincoln was strongly opposed to it. After the law passed in May 1854, Lincoln gave three public speeches, including a three-hour tract in Peoria, Illinois, summarizing his opposition to the expansion of slavery. These speeches helped to launch his political career. Lincoln said:

Little by little, but steadily as man's march to the grave, we have been giving up the old for the new faith. Nearly eighty years ago we began by declaring that all men are created equal; but now from that beginning we have run down to the other declaration, that for some men to enslave others is a "sacred right of self-government." These principles cannot stand together. They are as opposite as God and Mammon; and whoever holds to the one must despise the other.[7]

Violence erupted, slowing the plans for the railroad. Kansas, in particular, became a battleground over slavery. The North sent antislavery activists to sway the vote, while pro-slavery advocates from the neighboring slave state of Missouri crossed the border, too. Many of the antislavery settlers were Free Soilers, not against slavery but against the plantation system that hurt small farmers. People on both sides were armed. The state soon got the nickname "Bleeding Kansas," coined by New York City newspaper publisher Horace Greeley.

An abolitionist named John Brown led one violent episode. On May 24, 1856, Brown took several other men, including two of his sons, to a pro-slavery settlement on Pottawatomie Creek in southeastern Kansas. Five settlers were killed. These settlers did not actually own slaves but still supported the pro-slavery party. Brown was retaliating for an event that occurred three days earlier in which some 800 pro-slavery men had burned the antislavery settlement of Lawrence, Kansas. This would not be the last time the country heard from John Brown. Meanwhile, a new political party, determined to stop the expansion of slavery, was getting organized. With a strong antislavery platform, the Republican Party, which first met in February 1854, found many followers, including Abraham Lincoln.

The Mighty Ohio

On a hill above the Ohio River in the late 1830s, a lantern was hung on many nights in the upstairs window of a large brick house. When the lantern was lit, safety was promised inside the house that lay 300 feet (91 meters) up a steep path from the river. The house overlooking the river town of Ripley was owned by John Rankin, a Presbyterian minister and a fervent and fearless abolitionist. The glowing lantern signified that slave catchers were not nearby and that it was safe for runaway slaves crossing the river to climb the hill to Rankin's famous safe house on the Underground Railroad.

Rankin's house was one of hundreds of safe houses on the northern side of the Ohio River. From its source in Pittsburgh, Pennsylvania, the Ohio River flows westward along the southern borders of Ohio and Indiana to join the Mississippi River in Illinois. In the early nineteenth century, the river was a major

John Rankin was one of the most active "conductors" on the Underground Railroad. He and his family lived in a house in Ripley, Ohio, at the top of a 540-foot-high hill that looked over the Ohio River and the state of Kentucky. The Rankin family would light a lantern to signal to runaway slaves in Kentucky when it was safe to cross the river. Today the Rankin House *(top, left)* is a U.S. National Historic Landmark.

transportation route, filled with boats carrying people and cargo across the Midwest. The waters also marked the border between freedom and slavery, serving as the boundary between the free state of Ohio and the slave states of Virginia and Kentucky, and between Kentucky and the two free states of Indiana and Illinois. Jefferson Davis, then a senator from Mississippi, once told the Senate that slaves escaped from his state by hiding on northbound steamboats traveling up the Mississippi to the Ohio River. By crossing the Ohio River, slaves would be able to touch the land of freedom. The problem was how to get across.

CROSSING THE RIVER

Fugitive slaves swam the cold dark waters in summer and ventured over the ice in winter. Boarding ferries, they hid among the baggage or disguised themselves as servants or freed blacks. They were rowed and steered across by abolitionists and sympathizers. Some even found a small abandoned skiff and a pair of oars and rowed themselves. They always had to look behind them to see if they would be caught. Slave catchers in Kentucky could earn $100 for returning a slave to his or her owner. If the slave had crossed into Ohio or another state, the reward was about $200. That price was a good incentive to do whatever it took to catch a runaway slave.

Once they had arrived on the other side, the escaped slaves were still in grave danger. They had to quickly disappear from sight, because slave catchers roamed the harbors and streets along the riverbank. Fortunately for the fugitives, once they got to Ohio, Indiana, or Illinois, a network of people was waiting to help them in the river towns. By the 1830s, the Underground Railroad was growing in the Midwest, especially along the Ohio River. Abolitionist groups had formed and were determined to help fleeing slaves get across the Great Lakes to Canada.

Ohio had more than a dozen crossing points where the river was narrow and the Underground Railroad was in place to help fugitive slaves. The town of Ripley was one of the most well known. It was a busy place, with wagon makers, a clockmaker, wool and flour mills, and boatyards. Located about 50 miles (80 kilometers) east of Cincinnati, Ripley sits at a point where the Ohio River spans only about 1,000 feet (305 meters) across, according to Ann Hagedorn, author of *Beyond the River: The Untold Story of the Heroes of the Underground Railroad*. Because of its location, and the many abolitionists who lived there, Ripley was "a haven into which runaways seemed to disappear,"[1] she writes. Among the abolitionist leaders was John Rankin, a conductor on the Underground

Railroad. "I kept a depot on what was called the Underground railway," he later wrote. "It was so called because they who took passage on it disappeared from public view as really as if they had gone into the ground. After the fugitive slaves entered a depot on that road, no trace of them could be found."[2] The steps up to his house were nicknamed the "Freedom Stairway." Hundreds of slaves climbed those steps after crossing the river. Some nights, Rankin and his large family (he had more than 20 natural and adopted children) hid many slaves in the house. Jean, his wife, always had food waiting and a fire burning. One of his sons had a horse ready to take the fugitives to the next stop. Sometimes a runner would go off first, to let the next family know who was coming.

Rankin was born in Tennessee in 1793 to a family of Presbyterians who vehemently opposed slavery. He grew up as a serious, intensely spiritual young man, more and more concerned about slavery. When he became a minister, his Tennessee congregation forced him out because of his anti-slavery sermons. Rankin moved to Ripley, where he continued to preach against slavery and also write letters and articles and aid fugitive slaves. A series of Rankin's antislavery letters to his brother, who had purchased slaves, was published in news-papers and later in a book. In 1835, Rankin joined Ripley's small antislavery society with the Ohio antislavery organiza-tion and began to travel around the state, giving passionate public speeches decrying slavery as immoral and sinful. In many places, he was surrounded by angry mobs and attacked with stones and eggs. Once, an irate spectator hit him. "After all the argument I had just used to prove that all men should be free, it did seem as if some men were not fit for freedom,"[3] he wrote. But nothing stopped him from his life's purpose to end slavery.

Other well-known abolitionists also lived in Ripley, includ-ing John Parker, who helped hundreds of runaway slaves. Born to a white father and a slave mother, Parker grew up in slavery in Norfolk, Virginia. When he was eight, he was sold to a doctor in Alabama, who let him apprentice in an iron foundry and keep part of his pay. By the age of 18, he was able to buy his freedom. Eventually he moved north and settled in Ripley. A businessman and an inventor, Parker owned an iron foundry and made several successful inventions. His main line of work, though, was as an abolitionist. Sometimes he would even travel to Kentucky to help slaves escape. He often put his life on the line.

NORTH

Once fugitives passed through Ripley, they moved on along the secret safe routes that led from farm to town to farm all the way to Lake Erie, and then by boat across the Great Lake to Canada. From the banks of the Ohio River, they had to navigate some 250 miles (402 km) to get to the lake shore. With the help of abolitionists, the runaway slaves were hidden in carts or taken on horseback to the next town, often Red Oak. From there, they would travel to Russellville and then north to Sardinia, and then often to the farm of John M. Nelson, a friend of Rankin's. Some slaves were harbored in Quaker homes in New Petersburg.

If the fugitive slaves headed instead to Cincinnati, then they would go on to other towns, such as Lebanon and Springboro, according to Hagedorn. To the east, the town of Oberlin, along with Oberlin College, was a vital haven for runaway slaves. Both the town and college were founded in 1833 to educate ministers and teachers, and were dedicated to racial equality and the end of slavery. Black students were admitted to Oberlin College in 1834, and Frederick Douglass's daughter Rosetta would graduate from Oberlin. The Oberlin Anti-Slavery Society was founded in 1835 and had 300 members from its early days.

In Oberlin and other towns, abolitionists were waiting with a place to hide and words of encouragement. Sometimes the

Underground conductors sent coded notes ahead to let people know of the fugitives' impending arrival. "Dear Sir: By tomorrow's mail you will receive two volumes of the "Irrepressible

THE TRAGIC STORY OF MARGARET GARNER

In January 1856, a 23-year-old Kentucky slave named Margaret Garner, along with her husband, four children, and several other slaves, fled over the frozen Ohio River. In Cincinnati, they hid in a safe house owned by a freed slave. Slave catchers surrounded the house and demanded Garner and her family. Garner was desperate that her children not be captured back to slavery. She held a knife in her hand and shouted that she would rather her children die than be sent back to their slave owner. When the white men beat down the door, Garner killed her three-year-old daughter.

Garner and her husband were indicted on murder charges. But under the Fugitive Slave Act, a U.S. commissioner ordered the couple be released and returned to their owner, Archibald Gaines, a farmer in Boone County, Kentucky. A federal marshal took the Garners back to Kentucky. Meanwhile, Ohio governor Salmon P. Chase, who was a Republican and an abolitionist, demanded that the Kentucky governor return the Garners to Ohio to stand trial for murder. Abolitionists did not want to allow Kentucky slave owners to claim their runaway slaves in Ohio. Also, if the two were allowed to stand trial, they would be treated as any other citizens, rather than as slaves. Instead, Gaines sold the family to a man in New Orleans. On the way to New Orleans, the steamboat carrying the Garners collided with another boat. One of their children drowned in the accident. Garner died of typhoid fever in 1858. Inspired by Garner's tragic story, the author Toni Morrison wrote her novel *Beloved*, which won the Pulitzer Prize for Fiction in 1988.

Many safe houses had secret rooms, false floors, and openings that led to escape tunnels where runaway slaves hid. North Carolina slave Harriet Jacobs ran away from her master and hid for seven years in a crawl space above a storeroom in her grandmother's house. Pictured is the crawl space covered by sliding shelves in the home of Reverend Alexander Dobbin of Gettysburg, Pennsylvania.

Conflict" bound in black. After perusal, please forward and oblige,"[4] said one such note from Greene County, Ohio, as Hagedorn reports.

A BRICK HOUSE IN INDIANA

Indiana was established as a slave territory in 1800, led by a governor who owned slaves. But many settlers were against slavery, and when Indiana became a state in 1816, abolitionists controlled the legislature and approved a constitution banning slavery. Still, many settlers had moved to Indiana from slave states, and saw no problem with it. By the end of the 1840s, an active antislavery movement was in place. Many times, slaves crossed the Ohio River at Jeffersonville, Indiana, where Dr. Nathaniel Field, a medical doctor, preacher, and politician, was an organizer of the Underground Railroad. From there, runaway slaves went north and often were guided to a large brick house in Newport, where Levi Coffin and his wife, Catharine, were waiting with warm food.

The small town of Newport, which has been renamed Fountain City, lies about eight miles (13 km) from the Ohio border. Often the runaway slaves arrived at the Coffin house nearly starving, after days or even weeks and months of hiding in woods and barns from slave catchers. In the maid's room, a secret door opened to a crawl space between the walls, where 14 people could hide at one time. The Coffins fed and clothed them, sometimes letting them stay for weeks while they gained back their strength, and then sent them on their way to Canada. "Seldom had a week passed," Coffin recalled, "without our receiving passengers by this mysterious road. We found it necessary to be always prepared to receive such company and properly care for them."[5]

Like many Midwestern abolitionists, Coffin was a native Southerner. He was born in 1798, and as a young boy growing up in rural North Carolina, he saw slaves working in local farms and houses. His Quaker family did not own slaves, and he was raised to believe that slavery was wrong. "Both my parents and grandparents were opposed to slavery, and none of either of the families ever owned slaves; and all were friends of the oppressed, so I claim that I inherited my antislavery principles,"[6] Coffin wrote in his autobiography. One day while he was chopping wood with his father, he saw a group of slaves in handcuffs and chains being led down the road. His father told him that slave traders were going to sell them farther down south. The harsh image stuck with him. As a teenager, he helped a fugitive slave find shelter. Later, he ran a Sunday school where he taught slaves to read the Bible.

Seeking new possibilities in the frontier state of Indiana, Coffin and his wife moved north in 1826 and settled in the Quaker town of Newport. He opened a store and ran several endeavors, including a pork-cutting business. Coffin became a wealthy, respected member of the community. All the while, he never lost his hatred of slavery. He even made sure that he did not sell products that were produced by slave labor. He and Catharine opened their eight-room house to fugitive slaves. "I would invite them, in a low tone," said Coffin, "to come in, and they would follow me into the darkened house without a word, for we knew not who might be watching and listening."[7]

In some towns on the north banks of the Ohio River, free African Americans operated the Underground Railroad. Madison, Indiana, was a port city with a large pork industry in its brick warehouses along the river. The leader of the antislavery movement there was George DeBaptiste, born a free man in Virginia. He owned a barbershop, where he cut the hair of whites and blacks alike. He was devoted to helping slaves escape from across the river in Kentucky, as Bordewich writes. Often, he went to get them himself, and he used his own money to help them on their way. Kentucky slave owners were so angry at the success of DeBaptiste and his friends in Madison that, in 1846, they attacked their homes and nearly killed them. DeBaptiste had to move to Detroit, where he set up a new barbershop and bought a ship to take fugitives across the Detroit River. Since blacks were not allowed to pilot boats, he had to hire a white captain.

UNCLE TOM'S CABIN

One fugitive who crossed the Ohio River at Ripley was a young Kentucky slave named Eliza Harris, according to several accounts. Though her owners were not unkind, she and her baby were about to be sold separately, so she fled in desperation to the riverbank. The ice was breaking, but pursuers on horseback were close behind. "Clasping her babe . . . she sprang on to the first cake of ice, then from that to another and another. Sometimes the cake she was on would sink beneath her weight,"[8] Coffin writes. Safely on the other side, she was directed to the Rankin house. Later she stopped at Coffin's house in Indiana, where she recounted her story, and then went on safely to Ontario.

In 1852, inspired by Eliza's story and the stories of other fugitive slaves, a Connecticut abolitionist wrote a novel that shook up the country. The novel was *Uncle Tom's Cabin*, by Harriet Beecher Stowe. Born in 1811, Stowe was active in the abolitionist movement and had spent time in Cincinnati, listening to the stories of fugitive slaves. She also read the autobiography of Josiah Henson, a slave who had escaped his owner in Maryland to flee to Canada. Above all, she was angered by the Fugitive Slave Act of 1850.

In her dramatic novel, Stowe explored American slavery through characters that were larger than life. There was Tom, the devoutly religious slave who was sold down south to one owner after another. He saves a white girl, Eva, after she falls from a riverboat, and the two develop a strong bond based on their faith. Few characters in American literature are as cruel as Tom's last master, Simon Legree. Enraged by Tom's religion, Legree tries to break his spirit and ends up beating him to death. In another storyline, Eliza runs from the same master after she learns her son is to be sold. She meets up with her husband, who had also run away. In escaping a slave hunter, he almost kills the white man. Eliza, her husband, and son eventually escape to Canada and then to France and Liberia in Africa.

Stowe's story of the immorality and evil of slavery shocked many people and fed the abolitionist fervor. First serialized in the *Washington National Era*, an abolitionist newspaper, Beecher's masterpiece became the best-selling novel of the century. By 1857, some 2 million copies had been sold around the world. The story was also presented in theater and, later, films. *Uncle Tom's Cabin* incited outrage among those who favored slavery and deepened the resolve of abolitionists. Some people say that Stowe's novel contributed to the outbreak of the Civil War in 1861. The following year, President Abraham Lincoln invited Stowe to the White House. According to legend, he said to her, "So this is the little lady who made this big war?"[9]

DRED SCOTT

An important Supreme Court case in 1857 further stoked the debate over slavery. By the late 1850s, the United States was deeply divided both geographically and philosophically between slavery and freedom. All the Southern states allowed slavery. In contrast, the New England states had abolished slavery more than a half-century earlier. Vermont had outlawed slavery in 1777; Massachusetts in 1780; and New Hampshire in 1783. "All men are born free and equal, and have certain natural, essential, and inalienable rights,"[10] the Massachusetts Constitution stated in 1780. Pennsylvania passed a gradual emancipation act in 1780, and Rhode Island declared that all people born after March 1784 would be free. Connecticut and New York also allowed gradual abolition before permanently ending slavery. New Jersey was the last Northern state to end slavery in 1804 through gradual abolition, leaving some slaves in the state decades later. Slavery was not allowed in much of the Midwest, settled by antislavery pioneers from the South and East and lining up politically with New England.

There were 19 free states in 1859: Maine, Vermont, New Hampshire, Rhode Island, Connecticut, Massachusetts, New York, New Jersey, Pennsylvania, Ohio, Illinois, Indiana, Michigan, Minnesota, Wisconsin, Kansas, Iowa, Oregon, and California. The 15 slave states were: Texas, Louisiana, Arkansas, Alabama, Mississippi, Georgia, Florida, Tennessee, Kentucky, Delaware, Maryland, Virginia (including West Virginia), South Carolina, North Carolina, and Missouri. The Nebraska and Oklahoma territories also sanctioned slavery before the Civil War. Thus, the laws in the states varied when it came to blacks,

Dred Scott, who had traveled with his master to states where slavery was illegal, sued unsuccessfully for his freedom based on the Missouri Compromise. The case went up to the United States Supreme Court, which ruled against Scott. Scott's case further increased tensions between the North and the South.

both free and enslaved. When blacks crossed the borders between states that enforced different slave laws, their rights were not always clear.

For Dred Scott, a slave born in Virginia around 1799, the country's varied slavery laws became a crisis, which in turn led to a historic Supreme Court decision. Scott's owner, Dr. John Emerson, was an army officer who moved around. For a time, Scott lived with his owner in Wisconsin and Illinois, both free states. According to some state laws, Scott was no longer a slave after living in the free states. Other federal rulings, however, disputed this. The Missouri Compromise of 1820 stated that slave owners could bring slaves to free states and still retain their rights to ownership. The 1850 Fugitive Slave Act also asserted that owners had the right to retrieve slaves who fled to free states.

After Emerson died in 1843, Scott was hired out to another army officer. Finally, Scott decided to seek his freedom. First he offered to buy his freedom from Emerson's widow. When she refused, Scott took his case to court and sued her for his freedom. He believed that he should be free since he had lived for many years in free territory. The case went all the way to the Supreme Court as *Dred Scott v. Sanford*. Sanford was the name of the brother of Emerson's widow. In 1857, the court decided against Scott. Seven justices ruled that all blacks, both free and enslaved, could not be U.S. citizens and therefore did not have the right to sue in court or do anything else that citizens could do. Chief Justice Roger Taney stated in his decision that blacks were "so far inferior that they had no rights which the white man was bound to respect."[11] The ruling also did away with the Missouri Compromise's ban on slavery in territories north and west of the state of Missouri. For slaves and abolitionists, this decision was a huge setback.

JOHN BROWN'S RAID, 1859

While most abolitionists used speeches and newspapers to deliver their antislavery messages, some were driven to violence. Just after dusk on October 16, 1859, an abolitionist named John Brown and a group of 21 men crossed the Potomac River from

Maryland to Virginia. Brown, who had carried out violent attacks in the name of abolitionism in Kansas, plotted to capture weapons at the U.S. Arsenal in Harpers Ferry. He wanted to use the arms to attack the slavery system and start an "army of emancipation." His plan was to hide in the mountains and attack slave owners from there; he expected other slaves would run to join his forces. Brown's plan had been in the works for months. By this time, the fight against slavery had become so heated that even a desperate and violent idea like Brown's found followers. Abolitionists had sent him money. Even Harriet Tubman had expressed advice and support.

On that night, Brown led a group of sixteen whites and five blacks, including slaves, freed men, and fugitive slaves, and they were fearless. They cut the telegraph wires so that the townspeople could not call for help. They captured the armory, an arsenal, and a rifle plant before they took some 60 people hostage. But their plan was doomed to failure. A train that passed through Harpers Ferry notified authorities once it got to Baltimore. Federal troops rushed in. Brown took nine hostages and holed up at an engine house next to the armory. Many of Brown's followers were killed, including two of his sons. Some escaped to safety in Canada and the North, while Brown was wounded and captured. He was jailed in Charles Town, Virginia.

Brown stood trial for treason, murder, and conspiring with slaves to rebel. In a statement to the court, Brown said, "Now, if it is deemed necessary that I should forfeit my life, for the furtherance of the ends of justice, and mingle my blood further with the blood of my children, and with the blood of millions in this slave country, whose rights are disregarded by wicked, cruel, and unjust enactments—I say let it be done."[12] A jury convicted him on November 2, and Brown was sentenced to death. He maintained until the end that he had acted according to God's commandments. Virginia militia companies guarded Brown in case his followers tried to rescue him. On December 2, 1859, Brown was hanged.

ELECTION ON SLAVERY

John Brown's raid and its aftermath ignited fear and anger among slave owners and outrage in abolitionists. Virginia planters celebrated his execution, while in Massachusetts, the writer and philosopher Henry David Thoreau said, "This morning, Captain Brown was hung. He is not Old Brown any longer; he is an angel of light."[13] The episode was one more spark that would soon set the fire of civil war. The issue of slavery was increasingly tearing apart the nation.

The following year, voters went to the polls to express their views. The presidential election of 1860 was a referendum on slavery and the rights of states to determine their laws and destinies. The four presidential candidates offered differing views on slavery. Abraham Lincoln represented the new Republican Party, which was against the expansion of slavery but did not go as far as the abolitionists in demanding the end of slavery and asserting the equality of blacks and whites. The Democratic Party had split into Northern and Southern factions. Lincoln's rival, Illinois senator Stephen A. Douglas, represented the Northern Democrats; John C. Breckinridge, the incumbent vice president, represented the pro-slavery Southern Democrats; and John Bell of Tennessee was from the Constitutional Union Party, made up of people who supported neither the Democrats nor Republicans. In the end, Lincoln won a landslide majority in the Electoral College, but took less than 40 percent of the popular vote. None of the Southern states cast their votes for Lincoln.

War

The election of President Abraham Lincoln and the victory of his antislavery Republican Party in November 1860 raised fears in the Southern slave states. Southerners did not approve of the Republicans' desire for more federal control over state laws, industries, trade, and especially slavery. Lincoln had pledged not to abolish slavery immediately, but rather to stop its spread, but his antislavery views still threatened slave owners who felt that their way of life and independence would be jeopardized under his administration. By the time that Lincoln was inaugurated on March 4, 1861, seven Southern states had seceded, or pulled out of the United States of America, to form a separate government, the Confederate States of America, or the Confederacy. On April 12, the Civil War broke out when Confederate gunships bombarded and seized the federal Fort

Sumter in Charleston, South Carolina. Four more states soon joined the Confederacy.

The North went to war to reunite the country, while the Confederacy's aim was to be independent and continue the practice of slavery. Led by former Mississippi Senator Jefferson Davis, the Confederacy held to the belief that the people had a right to own slaves and to determine their destinies. Alexander H. Stephens, a Georgia lawyer and legislator who was vice president of the Confederacy, said that the cornerstone of the Confederate States "rests upon the great truth that the negro is not equal to the white man; that slavery—subordination to the superior race—is his natural and normal condition. This, our new government, is the first, in the history of the world, based upon this great physical, philosophical, and moral truth."[1] The population of the Confederate States was just over 9 million people, including some 3.5 million slaves. Another half-million slaves lived in border states that did not join the Confederacy— Delaware, Maryland, Kentucky, and Missouri. With the outbreak of war, American slaves saw reason for both hope and further despair. They saw that many Northerners who wanted to stop the spread of slavery did not want African Americans to achieve equality: Instead, they wanted the new western territories set aside for white settlers without slaves. There was no clear sign yet that the slaves would be freed.

SLAVERY IN WARTIME

The question of slavery was unresolved as the war began. Even the antislavery Republicans disagreed on whether to free the slaves immediately or to do it more slowly by stopping the expansion of slavery and gradually granting emancipation. Intent on uniting his country, Lincoln was cautious; he did not want to antagonize the border states, where slavery was still legal. At first the Union Army continued to follow the Fugitive Slave Act and returned runaway slaves to their owners.

CHARLESTON

MERCURY

EXTRA:

Passed unanimously at 1.15 o'clock, P. M. December 20th, 1860.

AN ORDINANCE

To dissolve the Union between the State of South Carolina and other States united with her under the compact entitled "The Constitution of the United States of America."

We, the People of the State of South Carolina, in Convention assembled, do declare and ordain, and it is hereby declared and ordained,

That the Ordinance adopted by us in Convention, on the twenty-third day of May, in the year of our Lord one thousand seven hundred and eighty-eight, whereby the Constitution of the United States of America was ratified, and also, all Acts and parts of Acts of the General Assembly of this State, ratifying amendments of the said Constitution, are hereby repealed; and that the union now subsisting between South Carolina and other States, under the name of "The United States of America," is hereby dissolved.

THE

UNION
IS
DISSOLVED!

As the war progressed and the South faced economic ruin, the Confederate states came to rely even more on the free labor of slaves to keep the economy afloat. Starting on April 19, 1861, the Union Navy began to blockade the Southern ports, disrupting the critical trade of cotton, tobacco, and other commodities. Without access to their harbors, Confederate troops also could not get fresh supplies. In the months that followed, Lincoln and his advisers saw that protecting slavery was supporting the Confederacy and hurting the Union war effort. On April 16, 1862, Lincoln signed a law freeing the slaves in Washington, D.C. The law compensated slave owners for their loss. A slave trader from Baltimore decided on the value of each slave, and the government paid compensation for 2,989 slaves.

In the upheaval of war, thousands of slaves escaped from their owners, both over the borders to the North and into parts of the South that had been captured and were occupied by federal soldiers. Norfolk, Virginia, strategically located on the Chesapeake Bay, surrendered to the Union Army in May 1862. Fugitive slaves from Virginia and other Southern states poured into Norfolk to live in freedom for the remainder of the war. The fugitive slaves were called "contraband," and the government was responsible to care for them, even setting up schools for the children. But in many contraband camps, the slaves were destitute and hungry, and the army did not have enough clothing, food, or even sanitation supplies for them. Thus, they continued to suffer, even in freedom. In some instances, soldiers mistreated the runaways, robbing and beating them.

(Opposite page) South Carolina was the first state to secede from the Union, on December 20, 1860. Ten other states followed, with Tennessee being the last to secede on June 8, 1861. The eleven states joined together to form the Confederate States of America. Above, in a special edition of the Charleston *Mercury*, South Carolina announces its secession from the Union.

Runaway slaves from Georgia cotton plantations and South Carolina rice farms walked for miles to get to the Union Army's Southern headquarters at Beaufort, South Carolina. They arrived barefoot and starving, often wearing only gunnysacks, in search of freedom and protection as well as food and shelter. One volunteer at the compound was Harriet Tubman, who had traveled south with other abolitionists to help in the war effort. She had been living in freedom in upstate New York but saw the war as a chance to fight slavery one more time. She cooked for the escaped slaves, nursed wounded soldiers, and even served as a backwoods spy for Union Army generals who needed help navigating the swamps and countryside. In one daring raid in 1863, Tubman led federal forces up the Combahee River on a Union Army boat to get supplies from Confederate farms and bases. Runaway slaves ran down from the woods to board the boat to freedom.

DARING ESCAPE

Slaves escaped to the safety of other federal warships. In September 1862, a 24-year-old slave named William Benjamin Gould fled from his owner in Wilmington, North Carolina, by rowing a boat with seven other slaves out to a Union gunboat called the *Cambridge*. Five days later, he began to serve on the gunboat and joined the U.S. Navy. He fought in the Navy for three years and kept a diary of his experiences.

One of the most daring wartime escapes of slaves occurred in the early morning of May 13, 1862, in Charleston Harbor. Robert Smalls, a 23-year-old slave, was a dockworker at the harbor. Smalls had worked on the harbor since he was a teenager, giving part of his wages to his owner. He knew how to rig boats, make sails, and even pilot a ship. He was skillful enough to become the helmsman of a Confederate military transport ship, the *Planter*. He also wanted his freedom. While the white officers of the boat went ashore that May night, Smalls and other black crewmen piloted the boat away. First they stopped

As a teenager, slave Robert Smalls worked down on the docks in Charleston, South Carolina. His knowledge of the Charleston Harbor later helped him and a small group of blacks, including his wife and children, to escape when he took a Confederate military transport ship and sailed toward the Union blockade. He provided valuable information to the Union Navy, and his actions became a major argument for allowing blacks to serve in the Union Army.

to pick up Smalls's wife and children and the relatives of the other men, hiding in wait on a wharf.

Smalls sailed the boat past Fort Sumter and four other Confederate forts guarding the harbor. The Union had blockaded the port with a fleet posted outside the harbor. Smalls raised a white flag and headed toward the federal ships. One ship, the USS *Onward*, almost fired at the *Planter* but saw the white flag just in time. The captain of the *Onward* quickly understood the situation. Smalls is reported to have said, "Good morning, sir! I have brought you some of the old United States' guns, sir!"[2] The slaves came out onto the deck. Smalls handed over the *Planter* and its cargo of explosives and ammunition to the U.S. Navy.

Not only had Smalls helped the Union by handing over the boat and its artillery, but he also gave the Navy information about the Confederate defenses. Smalls became famous for his fearlessness. "Is he not also a man—and is he not fit for freedom, since he made such a hazardous dash to gain it?"[3] asked an editorial in the New York *Daily Tribune*. Lincoln signed a bill that gave Smalls and the other men a prize ($1,500 for Smalls) for capturing the Confederate ship. In August 1862, Smalls went to Washington, D.C, to try to persuade Lincoln and War Secretary Edwin Stanton to allow black men to fight with the Union. Smalls later became the first black captain of a U.S. Navy vessel. After the Civil War and the passage of the Fourteenth Amendment, which granted citizenship to African Americans, Smalls entered politics and served five terms as a congressman from South Carolina.

EMANCIPATION PROCLAMATION

Lincoln's aim was to reunite the country and save the Union. As such, he did not want to lose the loyalty of the border slave states that had not severed ties to the federal government. But abolitionists like Frederick Douglass pushed for the war to focus on ending slavery. "Any attempt now to separate the freedom of the slave from the victory of the government, any attempt now to secure peace to the whites while leaving the blacks in chains, will be labor lost,"[4] Douglass said in May 1861. As the war entered its second year, abolitionists awaited a definitive sign that slavery would end. Finally, Lincoln took an important step. On September 22, 1862, Lincoln issued a first draft of the Emancipation Proclamation, a wartime order that would free the slaves in the Confederacy. The final document was ready by the end of the year. The night before the proclamation was to be issued on January 1, 1863, Douglass and others gathered in the telegraph office in Boston. "We were waiting and listening as for a bolt from the sky, which should rend the fetters of four million slaves; we were watching, as it were, by the dim light of the stars, for the dawn of a new day; we were longing for the answer to the agonizing prayers of centuries,"[5] Douglass recalled.

The Emancipation Proclamation marked a turning point in the war's purpose. It read, in part: "That on the first day of January in the year of our Lord 1863, all persons held as slaves within any State or designated part of a State . . . in rebellion against the United States, shall be then, thenceforward, and forever free."[6] But the wartime order was just a beginning. Since only Confederate territory was included in the order, slavery continued in Kentucky, Maryland, Delaware, Missouri, and West Virginia, a fact that angered impatient abolitionists. Nonetheless, the majority of the nation's 4 million slaves were now freed.

Douglass and others also pushed Lincoln to allow black men to fight in the Union Army and Navy. In July 1862, Congress had voted to let blacks join the military but only as laborers, scouts, nurses, and other workers, not soldiers. The Emancipation Proclamation directed that black soldiers would be accepted in the armed forces. Black regiments and units were formed, yet the soldiers were not trained or equipped as well as whites and were paid much less. Even so, Lincoln faced criticism from Kentucky and other border states for allowing blacks to fight. Slave owners in Kentucky did not want their slaves to be recruited as soldiers, but Lincoln defended his decision. "If slavery is not wrong, nothing is wrong. . . . And yet I have never understood that the Presidency conferred upon me an unrestricted right to act officially upon this judgment and feeling. . . . I claim not to have controlled events, but confess plainly that events have controlled me," Lincoln wrote to Kentucky newspaper editor A.G. Hodges on April 4, 1864.[7]

Thus, runaway slaves could now gain their freedom by fighting for the Union. In Massachusetts, Douglass helped to recruit soldiers for the first black unit, the Massachusetts 54th Regiment. His sons Lewis and Charles joined up as well. The interracial 54th Regiment fought bravely at Fort Wagner, South Carolina, on July 18, 1863, where its white general, an

THE BLACK DISPATCHES

Several African-American spies made significant contributions to the Union war effort. Most have been forgotten, their names lost and their deeds unrecognized. Harriet Tubman was well known for her spying trips in the backwoods of South Carolina. Less well known was Mary Touvestre of Norfolk, Virginia. Touvestre was a freed slave employed as a housekeeper by a Confederate engineer. The engineer had the job of repairing a federal ship and making it into a Confederate ironclad warship, the *Virginia*. When she heard the engineer talk about plans for the ship to be used to battle against the Northern blockade of the Norfolk port, she stole a set of the ship's plans. Taking huge risks, Touvestre secretly traveled from Norfolk to Washington, D.C., where she gave the plans to the Department of the Navy. Because of her information, the Navy hurried to finish building its own ironclad ship, the USS *Monitor*. The *Virginia* destroyed two Union warships and ground another before the *Monitor* was ready to

abolitionist named Robert Gould Shaw, was killed in battle. By the war's end, some 186,000 African-American men had fought in the Union Army. Most were runaways from the South and border states. They also fell on the battlefield— 38,000 were killed or wounded. In the Confederacy, blacks were kept out of the army until the very end. One founder of the Confederacy, Georgia political leader Howell Cobb, is said to have declared, "If slaves make good soldiers, our whole theory of slavery is wrong."[8]

PEACE AND TRAGEDY

For four long years, the nation was at war. More than 3 million soldiers fought, and some 620,000 died in the war that turned

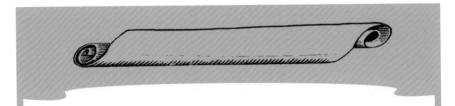

launch. But the Monitor was eventually able to prevent the *Virginia* from opening the port of Norfolk to supplies from Europe.

Another Civil War spy was John Scobell, an educated slave from Mississippi who had been freed by his owner. He was recruited as an agent by the army's chief of intelligence, Allan Pinkerton, owner of the famous Chicago detective agency. Pinkerton hired Scobell to take on different identities to get behind Confederate lines and bring back information. Scobell pretended to be a cook, laborer, or servant while he went on missions into Virginia. He was able to get information on Confederate supplies, troop movements, and battle plans. He often went into the black communities, where people were willing to tell him what they knew of the local Confederate activity. Scobell was also a member of a secret black antislavery organization in the South, known as the "Legal League." Members of the league helped carry information from Scobell to Union officers.

much of the South into bloodstained battlefields. Along with the high numbers of casualties came economic disaster. Cities and towns, such as Columbia, South Carolina, and Atlanta, Georgia, were left in ruins. Cotton and tobacco fields were burned and turned barren. Small farms and large plantations had fallen to rubble. The war ended slavery and reunited the country; it also strengthened the role of the federal government, but the damage done left much bitterness and despair across the South.

Just days after Confederate general Robert E. Lee surrendered to Union general Ulysses S. Grant and the Civil War's end was near, the nation was shaken by yet another tragedy. On April 14, 1865, President Lincoln and his wife, Mary Todd Lincoln, were attending a play, *Our American Cousin*, at Ford's Theatre in Washington, D.C. Lincoln's aides had warned him against going out that night, fearing a rebel might want to shoot him because of the unsettled political situation, but he went anyway. After the curtain rose, an unemployed actor and Confederate sympathizer, John Wilkes Boothe, entered the president's theater box and raised a derringer pistol. He shot Lincoln in the back of his head.

Lincoln died the next day, sending the nation into shock and mourning. "Our Great Loss," stated the headline of *The New York Times* on April 16, 1865. "Death of President Lincoln. The Songs of Victory Drowned in Sorrow." Across the country, people draped their homes in black. "The great grief is still uppermost in all hearts, and its signs are apparent on every hand. Every yard of black fabric in the city on Saturday was bought up at an early hour,"[9] one reporter in Washington, D.C., wrote. On April 21, his coffin left the capital on a train bound for Springfield, Illinois. Thousands of people waited along the railroad tracks as the funeral train slowly traveled 1,654 miles (2,662 kilometers), through 180 cities, on the way back home, a sad echo of Lincoln's earlier journey to the White House in February 1861.

SLAVERY FINALLY ENDS

During his lifetime, Lincoln worried that the Emancipation Proclamation was a wartime order that was not sufficient to end slavery, even with a Union victory. Before his assassination, Lincoln and others sought a constitutional amendment to outlaw slavery permanently. As the Civil War drew to a close, on February 1, 1865, Lincoln signed the Thirteenth Amendment abolishing slavery. His signature was not required, but he gave it anyway. Nearly seven months after his death, on December 6, 1865, the twenty-seventh state ratified the amendment, making it official. In part, the amendment states: "Neither slavery nor involuntary servitude, except as a punishment for crime whereof the party shall have been duly convicted, shall exist within the United States, or any place subject to their jurisdiction."[10] The amendment freed the remaining slaves in Kentucky and Delaware, the last two border states still allowing slavery. The other border states had already outlawed slavery. New Jersey also had a small number of slaves who were now freed.

Further steps toward racial equality came with the Fourteenth Amendment, adopted in 1868, which overruled the Supreme Court's *Dred Scott* decision that had denied blacks the right to be citizens. States were now required to provide all citizens equal protection under the law. In 1870, Congress adopted the Fifteenth Amendment prohibiting government from denying a person the right to vote because of race, color, or previous condition of slavery. Black men now had the right to vote; women of any race were not included.

GOING HOME

Just as the Underground Railroad was only a first step to freedom, the war's end did not ease the struggles of freed slaves. In the years that followed, African Americans faced not only prejudice and segregation, but also economic inequality and new challenges—poorly equipped schools, unemployment, poverty, and hunger. After the war, Harriet Tubman went

On April 19, 1866, nearly 5,000 African-American citizens assembled at the White House to celebrate the abolition of slavery. Marching past 10,000 cheering spectators, the crowd proceeded up Pennsylvania Avenue to Franklin Square for religious services and speeches by prominent politicians, such as President Andrew Johnson. A sign on top of the speaker's platform read: "We have received our civil rights. Give us the right to suffrage and the work is done."

home to Auburn, New York. Traveling through New Jersey in 1865, a conductor tried to remove her from the train because of her race—one more insult to a woman who had served the Union Army. Many members of Tubman's family had settled in Auburn, and she owned a small house there. The tolerant and diverse community included Quakers and abolitionists and friends of Tubman. Her first husband, John, was killed in 1867 in Dorchester County, Maryland. In 1869, she married Nelson Davis, who had fought with black regiments in the Civil War.

With the same devotion she had poured into the Underground Railroad, Tubman turned to fighting for the women's suffrage movement, education for black children, and housing and jobs for freed slaves. Every week, former slaves would knock at her door, looking for food and shelter. The older men and women were especially desperate, as they had no way to support themselves after a life of slavery and no savings. Many of them, like Tubman, were still illiterate. Tubman was finally able to open the Harriet Tubman Home for the Aged, a home for elderly former slaves, where she herself was staying at her death in 1913.

Meanwhile, Frederick Douglass had gained the confidence of President Lincoln during his lifetime. He had moved to Washington, D.C., and advised him on matters relating to slavery and African Americans during the war. Even though the two did not always agree, and Douglass was impatient with Lincoln's unwillingness to abolish slavery immediately, they respected each other greatly. After Lincoln's death, Douglass mourned with the rest of the nation. To honor her husband's admiration of Douglass, Lincoln's widow, Mary Todd Lincoln, sent the former slave a remembrance: the president's favorite walking stick. After the war, Douglass continued to speak out on issues relating to civil rights. He served as a city official in Washington, D.C., and the minister to the republic of Haiti before his death in 1895.

The nation's memories of the Underground Railroad were fading fast. William Still gathered his notes and letters from fugitive slaves and abolitionists to write a book. Still's *The Underground Railroad*, first published in 1872, is a masterful chronicle of the runaway slaves who came through Philadelphia and one of few primary records of the era. Slave narratives, the autobiographical stories written by slaves, also offered glimpses into the travails of runaway slaves. Yet much of the Underground Railroad had been secret and hidden. If this crucial piece of the nation's history was to really become known, the task lay with future generations.

A Slave Named
Hadizatou

The Underground Railroad is now seen as one of the boldest moments in America's history. But the efforts of the fugitive slaves and abolitionists to help runaways escape from bondage and achieve freedom were not always considered to be noble. Since protecting runaway slaves meant breaking the law and putting people in danger, most did not make their actions public. Runaway slaves rarely told their stories of sneaking past the plantation gates and trudging through dark woods. Though some abolitionists touted the Underground Railroad, Frederick Douglass and others thought it best to keep quiet and avoid inviting danger to those involved. After the Civil War, families found that their mother or uncle would not say exactly what they did for the Underground Railroad or describe how their father or cousin found their way to freedom. Those who had risked everything to fight slavery were used to keeping secrets. Even when there was nothing more to fear, they still did not want to talk about what had happened. What historic records did survive were often passed down in families and lost to later generations.

Several abolitionists and slaves did write memoirs of their experiences. Levi Coffin's 732-page autobiography, *Reminiscences of Levi Coffin*, published in 1876, detailed his experiences helping slaves escape through Indiana. The black abolitionist William Still's chronicles of fugitive slaves coming through Philadelphia revealed valuable and unforgettable details of escapes. Frederick Douglass was one of several slaves who wrote narratives of their lives in captivity and described their flights to freedom.

Then in the 1890s, a history professor in Ohio undertook a major research project on the Underground Railroad. Wilbur H. Siebert, who taught American history at Ohio State University, enlisted his students to help research the Underground Railroad in Ohio and other states as a way to get them interested in history. They were able to interview aging abolitionists, runaway slaves, and their descendants, and to gather letters, newspaper clippings, and other primary documents. His book, *The Underground Railroad: From Slavery to Freedom*, was published by Macmillan Company in 1898. After the book was finished, Siebert continued his research project, now stored at the Ohio Historical Society in Columbus, consisting of some 5,000 documents. Siebert's collection of stories and histories is a vital contribution not just to the history of the Underground Railroad but to that of the whole antebellum era. Yet despite his painstaking research and interviews with hundreds of people, he was also swept away by myth and hearsay. It was sometimes not possible to separate fact from fiction.

A SPIRIT REIGNITED

The Underground Railroad had grown into a national myth by the middle of the twentieth century. Most people learned

THE

UNDERGROUND RAIL ROAD.

A RECORD

OF

FACTS, AUTHENTIC NARRATIVES, LETTERS, &C.,

Narrating the Hardships Hair-breadth Escapes and Death Struggles

OF THE

Slaves in their efforts for Freedom,

AS RELATED

BY THEMSELVES AND OTHERS, OR WITNESSED BY THE AUTHOR;

TOGETHER WITH

SKETCHES OF SOME OF THE LARGEST STOCKHOLDERS, AND

MOST LIBERAL AIDERS AND ADVISERS,

OF THE ROAD.

BY

WILLIAM STILL,

For many years connected with the Anti-Slavery Office in Philadelphia, and Chairman
of the Acting Vigilant Committee of the Philadelphia Branch of
the Underground Rail Road.

Illustrated with 70 fine Engravings by Bensell, Schell and others, and
Portraits from Photographs from Life.

Thou shalt not deliver unto his master the servant that has escaped from his master unto thee.—*Deut*. xxiii. 15.

SOLD ONLY BY SUBSCRIPTION.

PHILADELPHIA:

PORTER & COATES,

822, CHESTNUT STREET.

1872.

about it in brief paragraphs in American history books or in children's books that told dramatic stories of Harriet Tubman and fictionalized tales of runaway slaves. Much of what was written was based only loosely on known facts. For example, the role of Quakers and other white abolitionists was over-emphasized, while the importance of black abolitionists and the slaves themselves, who often fled from slavery alone and without any help, went unheralded. Even Tubman's story was blurred by well-meaning exaggerations that made her larger than life, while neglecting some details that showed her to be even more heroic. For instance, people wrote that she had saved hundreds of slaves, when she probably brought about 70 to freedom. Yet little was known about her family, her life during the Civil War, and other acts of courage.

The civil rights movement of the 1950s and 1960s sparked new interest in African-American history, including the Underground Railroad. For nearly a century after slavery's abolition, Jim Crow laws separated the races and prejudicial attitudes created a second-class nation for African Americans in much of the South. Outside the South, they were also dis-criminated against, kept out of voting booths, segregated in disadvantaged neighborhoods, and denied decent housing, education, and jobs. Through brave actions mirroring the abolitionists' activities before the Civil War, civil rights activ-ists pushed the courts and local and federal governments to end segregation, tear down Jim Crow, and open the doors

(Opposite page) **William Still, often called "The Father of the Underground Railroad," helped about 60 slaves per month escape from slavery. He recorded the stories of 649 fugitives, which was later published in a book called *The Underground Rail Road*. During one of his interviews, Still discovered that a runaway was his own brother Peter, from whom he had been separated since childhood.**

to new opportunities. On August 28, 1963, the civil rights leader Martin Luther King Jr. stood on the steps of the Lincoln Memorial and gave his famous "I Have a Dream" speech. "Now is the time to make real the promises of democracy. Now is the time to rise from the dark and desolate valley of segregation to the sunlit path of racial justice. Now is the time to lift our nation from the quicksands of racial injustice to the solid rock of brotherhood. Now is the time to make justice a reality for all of God's children,"[1] said King, echoing Douglass and others who came before.

An important effort during this time was the drive to end segregation on public transportation, such as buses and trains. As during the Underground Railroad, the symbolism of the journey to freedom caught the public consciousness during the Freedom Rides of the early 1960s. Civil rights activists boarded buses and trains in North Carolina and other southern states, insisting on being seated and in any seat they chose, despite laws allowing segregation of the races. On December 1, 1955, when the seamstress and activist Rosa Parks refused to give up her seat to a white man on a city bus in Montgomery, Alabama, she sparked the year-long Montgomery bus boycott. The boycott led to a Supreme Court decision declaring that segregation on city transit systems was unconstitutional.

People began to try to get closer to the Underground Railroad. In 1984, *National Geographic* magazine published a groundbreaking story on the railroad, including maps, interviews, and photographs that sparked enormous interest. In 1996, a young college student from Maryland named Anthony Cohen undertook an 800-mile (1,287-km) journey, retracing the steps of a fugitive slave on the Underground Railroad. He walked from Montgomery County, Maryland, to Ontario, Canada, and recorded the journey with notes and photographs. Later he published his experiences in *Smithsonian* magazine and in a book. Historians and authors undertook new investigations of the people and places in the so-called network of freedom.

Many contemporary researchers have worked hard to separate myth from reality in understanding the antislavery efforts before the Civil War. "Although the Underground Railroad was a reality, much of the material relating to it belongs in the realm of folklore rather than history,"[2] writes Larry Gara in his 1996 book *The Liberty Line: The Legend of the Underground Railroad.* He especially deplores the lack of attention given to the slaves' own role in escaping captivity and the focus on the abolitionist as the hero of the Underground Railroad. Social historians and archaeologists gathered funding for new independent research, and scholars combed through birth records, letters, old newspapers, and advertisements. Several biographers, especially Kate Clifford Larson, Catherine Clinton, and Jean M. Humez, broke ground in their studies of Harriet Tubman. They used newspapers, diaries, oral histories, and official records to explore the American heroine and helped renew attention to the woman who overcame such enormous odds to help so many others.

As they dug into the past, historians and biographers found plenty of documentation about the Underground Railroad, from newspaper clippings to slave narratives, diaries, and abolitionist pamphlets, that helped shine new light on its previously murky history. Author Fergus M. Bordewich wrote *The Underground Railroad and the War for the Soul of America,* a book full of stories that had been buried or forgotten. Ann Hagedorn's book *Beyond the River: The Untold Story of the Heroes of the Underground Railroad* brought to life the tumultuous and productive abolitionist movement along the Ohio River.

QUILT CODE CONTROVERSY

Recent research has uncovered new information about the Underground Railroad. For example, rather than the Underground Railroad leading a great number of slaves to freedom, those who made it safely to the North were only a small percentage of the 4 million American slaves before the Civil War;

and many who fled their owners never found freedom. Now researchers are reluctant to even put a number on those who escaped on the railroad. Also, rather than the runaway slave being a passive recipient of the white abolitionist's generos-

MYTH-BUSTER

Giles R. Wright Jr. devoted his life to the history of African Americans in New Jersey—and that meant he had to clear up a lot of misinformation about the Underground Railroad. For nearly 30 years before his death at the age of 73 in 2009, the historian directed the Afro-American History Program at the New Jersey Historical Commission. He wrote a book on the history of African Americans in New Jersey and received a state grant to develop a comprehensive history of the runaway slaves who came through New Jersey. A graduate of Georgetown University, with a master's degree in African Studies from Howard University, the New Jersey native wanted students and adults to learn more about the lives of African Americans in the state. But when it came to the Underground Railroad, he believed that it was too easy to romanticize a time in history when blacks and whites cooperated. "There is no aspect of black American history that is more popular—or more shrouded in misrepresentation, speculation, fabrication, and myth,"* Wright said of the railroad.

People who think they live in or own an Underground Railroad site are reluctant to believe otherwise, even in the face of documented evidence to the contrary, he said. In the early 2000s, Wright learned of a bar in Central New Jersey, whose owner mistakenly claimed that thousands had passed through its crawl spaces on the Underground Railroad and even took donations from visitors. But Wright could not find any evidence that the building was indeed

ity, hundreds of freed and enslaved African Americans who risked their lives to help slaves were an important bedrock of the Underground Railroad. On both sides of the borders, African-American men and women, most of whom will never

used as a safe house. "Unfortunately, a number of myths about the Underground Railroad have come into existence over the years,"** he said, comparing it to the popular claim that "Washington slept here." Wright also fought against misinformation about the numbers of slaves who traveled the railroad. "Slaves who ran away and came north constituted a very small percentage of the overall number of slaves who ran away. Most runaways stayed in the South and did not come north,"*** he said.

When a book was published in 1999 about a secret code system using the patterns on handmade quilts to pass information about escaping on the Underground Railroad, Wright spoke out publicly against it. He saw that educators were teaching schoolchildren about the quilts, and museums were hosting Underground Railroad quilt exhibitions; meanwhile, historians had found no real evidence of the quilt codes. "It is a perfect example of what those of us who are attempting to do serious Underground Railroad research are up against,"† Wright said.

---

*Hoag Levins, "New Jersey's Underground Railroad Myth-Buster," Historic Camden County, June 4, 2001. Available online. URL: http://historic camdencounty.com/ccnews11.shtml.
** Brian T. Murray, "Giles R. Wright Jr., Renowned Scholar of African American History, Dies at 73." *Newark Star-Ledger*, Feb. 5, 2009. Available online. URL: http://www.nj.com/news/index.ssf/2009/02/giles_r_ wright_jr_renowned_sch.html.
***Levins, "New Jersey's Underground Railroad Myth-Buster."
†Ibid.

be known by name, helped fugitives by providing shelter, food, guidance, and other assistance.

One recent controversy has been over the so-called quilt codes. For a long time, some people thought that slaves sewed patterns into quilts with secret messages about the Underground Railroad. Quilt block designs such as the "North Star" and "Wagon Wheel" were thought to contain directions for fugitives on their journeys to freedom. In 1999, Jacqueline Tobin and Raymond Dobard wrote about quilt codes and other clandestine communications in their book *Hidden in Plain View: A Secret Story of Quilts and the Underground Railroad*. Tobin had met an African-American woman in South Carolina who told her about quilts with secret codes in her family. Others besides Tobin had suggested that, before the Civil War, slaves hung quilts in their yards—with specific patterns or hung in a special way—to signify whether it was safe for runaway slaves to stop there.

Many children's picture books, museum exhibits, and other media have also celebrated quilt codes. But historians have so far found little evidence that handmade slave quilts held hidden messages about the Underground Railroad. Many scholars of African-American history criticize the idea for taking away from the real history. "What better way to teach children about slavery than by dressing the story up all cute and pretty with quilt patterns and kindly folks who used them to guide runaways to freedom—then we don't have to talk about the realities of slavery, and of running away, etc. It seems to me to be part and parcel of the continued erasure of African-American history—by creating mythical stories the truth is eventually lost,"[3] Tubman biographer Kate Clifford Larson said.

Likewise, the old song "Follow the Drinking Gourd" was once thought to have been sung to guide runaway slaves to safety. The song is about the North Star, found near the Big Dipper constellation that is also known as the Drinking Gourd. But researchers discovered that the song was first published in

1928 and made famous by the Weavers, a folk group, in the late 1940s. It is not likely that slaves could have sung the song. "Few aspects of the American past have inspired more colorful mythology than the Underground Railroad. . . . But faked history serves no one, especially when it buries important truths that have been hidden far too long,"[4] Bordewich wrote in *The New York Times* in 2007.

A NATIONAL TREASURE

Federal recognition and funding have helped lift the Underground Railroad from a sidebar in history textbooks to a highlight of the nation's human story. On July 21, 1998, President Bill Clinton signed a bill to help preserve and protect the Underground Railroad, recognizing it as a national treasure like the Statue of Liberty and the Lincoln Memorial. The bill known as the National Underground Railroad Network to Freedom Act authorized the National Park Service to link the sites of the Underground Railroad, produce educational programs for the public, and forge new partnerships to commemorate the historic escape route. The law came with federal funding to spearhead new activity and protect more than 300 sites and programs around the country and the Virgin Islands. A private organization, Friends of the Network to Freedom Association, formed in 2006 to support the park service's programs by organizing conferences and funding research. Still, the funding for these efforts remains precarious and their future is not certain.

In 2004, the National Underground Railroad Freedom Center opened in Cincinnati. The modern museum, situated not far from the banks of the Ohio River, is devoted to telling the story of the fugitive slaves' flights to freedom and keeping alive the history of the abolitionist movement. At the same time, the museum is determined to help end the tragedy of modern-day slavery by letting the public know what is happening around the world now. Also in 2004, the Friends of the Underground Railroad Inc., a private charitable organization supporting the

In August 2004, about 280,000 people celebrated the opening of the National Underground Railroad Freedom Center in Cincinnati, Ohio. Since then visitors have come from around the world to tour the exhibits and attend educational programs. The goal of the center is to tell the stories of the Underground Railroad and to help spread awareness about modern-day slavery issues.

preservation and recognition of the Underground Railroad, was founded.

Under the umbrella of the National Park Service, state and local historical societies, scholars, and private organizations try to map the safe houses and hiding places on the Underground Railroad. One of their challenges is separating fact from fiction. The National Park Service has a lengthy documentation process to verify sites. Judith Wellman, vice president of Friends of the Underground Railroad and professor of history emerita at the State University of New York, developed the Wellman Scale to rate Underground Railroad sites on their authenticity. From a level five's "conclusive evidence of involvement" to level one's "probably not true; reason to doubt,"[5] the scale helps determine how likely it is that a site was part of the Underground Railroad. It is not easy to verify the authenticity of the history of an old house or even a public building like a church. Documentation is lacking even for famous sites. In some cases, buildings thought to have been part of the Underground Railroad have not been verified.

The importance of documenting history becomes apparent when a building is threatened with demolition, as happened in Brooklyn, New York. Six buildings on Duffield Street in downtown Brooklyn had long been considered to be the sites of abolitionist activity. The city, however, wanted to demolish the buildings to create a green space for the newly developed neighborhood with plans for new hotels and businesses. City officials investigated and found no hard evidence that the buildings were in fact part of the Underground Railroad. Local preservationists and advocates of African-American history lobbied to save at least one building at 227 Duffield Street, once the home of abolitionists Thomas Truesdell and his wife, Harriet Lee Truesdell. He worked for William Lloyd Garrison's abolitionist newspaper, and she was an officer in a woman's antislavery society. In early 2009, the city agreed not to condemn the building. Advocates hope that 227 Duffield Street will become an Underground Railroad museum.

RIDING THE RAILROAD BY BIKE

With the renewed interest in the journeys of fugitive slaves, a bicycle touring organization in 2007 mapped out a 2,008-mile (3,232-km) Underground Railroad Bicycle Route. The nonprofit Adventure Cycling Association partnered with the University of Pittsburgh's Center for Minority Health to trace the various paths that runaway slaves took to freedom. Starting in Mobile, Alabama, where slaves arrived on boats from Africa, and heading north, bicyclists can follow routes through Alabama, Mississippi, Tennessee, and Kentucky. The routes cross the Ohio River and head up through the state of Ohio to Lake Erie. Several loops circle Ohio, including a one-day trip through Ripley, the river town famous for its abolitionist history.

To enter Canada, bicyclists can cross the Peace Bridge in Buffalo, New York, and follow the shore of Lake Ontario. Pedalers complete their journey at Owen Sound, a town where fugitive slaves settled, located on the shores of Georgian Bay, a large bay that is part of Lake Huron in Ontario. The online maps can be downloaded. Bicyclists can take short day trips or longer treks that cover many miles, just as the slaves did.

CONTROVERSY AND INSPIRATION

The Underground Railroad continues to inspire, and even to raise controversy. For example, some people believe that plantations and slave quarters should be considered a part of the Underground Railroad network and history because those were the places where slaves started their journeys. Others feel that only safe houses and routes that celebrate the antislavery spirit and quest for freedom should be recognized as part of the Underground Railroad.

Even the historic figure of Harriet Tubman still stirs up varying opinions. In 2008, a new sculpture of Tubman was placed in a plaza in Harlem, the predominately African-American neighborhood in northern Manhattan. The sculptor positioned the 10-foot-high (3-meter-high) bronze statue so that Tubman is facing south. An outcry arose when people realized which direction she was facing. They could not understand why the sculptor did not want her to face north, away from slavery, and the direction that she headed on her brave journeys on the Underground Railroad. "We hate what they did. It is just an outrage," said Jacob Morris, director of the Harlem Historical Society. The sculptor insisted, however, that she wanted Tubman facing south. "She's best known for her sojourns north but what is most impressive to me are her trips south, where she risked her own freedom,"[6] the sculptor, Alison Saar, said. The statue is in the Harriet Tubman Memorial Plaza at the intersection of Frederick Douglass Boulevard, St. Nicholas Avenue, and 122nd Street.

MODERN-DAY SLAVERY

More than 100 years after Frederick Douglass and Harriet Tubman walked to freedom with the help of the Underground Railroad, Hadizatou Mani was sold into slavery in the North African country of Niger. She was 12 years old. Her price was $500. "I was negotiated over like a goat,"[7] she said later. Niger has a caste system, which divides up society by people's inherited social status and offers little opportunity for people to escape their parents' fates. Mani was born into the slave caste, and her mother was also a slave. Not yet a teenager, Mani was sold to a 60-year-old man who beat her, made her work in the fields, and forced her to bear him three children. After many years, Mani was able to negotiate her freedom, though she had to spend six months in prison for defying her owner, who called himself her husband.

Though slavery was outlawed in Niger in 2003, just as it has been outlawed in virtually every modern nation, the practice continues there and around the globe in the twenty-first century. According to Free the Slaves, an advocacy organization in Washington, D.C., that seeks to end slavery and restore the lives of former slaves, there were 27 million slaves in the world in 2009. This number includes people forced to work under the threat of violence and unable to get away. "Despite the official abolition of slavery, racism still pollutes our world. So too do contemporary forms of slavery, including bonded servitude, forced prostitution, and the use of children in warfare and the international drug trade. It is essential that we speak out loud and clear against such abuses,"[8] said United Nations Secretary-General Ban Ki-moon in 2009.

Modern slavery is not the same as the slavery that existed in the United States before the Civil War. Today most slaves are controlled not by the laws and social contracts that allowed American slaves to be bought and sold without recourse. Rather, today's slaves are tied by debts and through contracts to people who need cheap labor. They are not necessarily of a certain race or ethnic group. Instead, they are desperately poor, without land or property, and thus vulnerable to people who prey on them, their children, and their families. Among the many disturbing facts about modern-day slavery is that the value of the individual slave has fallen dramatically. According to Free the Slaves, the cost of slaves was historically quite expensive—around $40,000 in today's currency. Yet today a slave costs an average of about $90 in much of the world. This steep drop in value means that slaves are even more disposable than in the past—a dangerous fact that makes slaves' lives even more perilous and dispensable.

Slavery today exists in many forms, according to Anti-Slavery International, the United Kingdom-based nonprofit organization. Under bonded labor, people take out a loan and are forced to repay the debt by working long days, possibly for years; often they are never able to pay off the loan. The loan may even be passed down to their children. Forced labor occurs when people are recruited to work under a threat of violence or other penalties. Their bosses can be individuals or even governments. Trafficking refers to the trade and transport of women, children, and men, often across national borders, to force them into slavery. Some modern-day slaves are born into slavery and inherit the status. In other cases, like Mani's, women and young girls are forced by violence and coercion into marriages and lives of servitude to their husbands.

CHILD SLAVERY

Children make up as much as half of the global slave industry. Even more children are working under poor conditions, though not slavery. Child labor affects some 158 million children ages five to fourteen, or one in six children in the world, according to the United Nations Children's Fund (UNICEF), an agency of the United Nations. Not all children who work are slaves, but most are underpaid and do work that is often hazardous to their health. The labor prevents them from going to school so that they could have a better future. Yet the money they earn is important to their families, who might otherwise starve or lose their shelter. For example, outside Recife, a coastal town in northern Brazil, children search through the Olinda trash dump to find bottles and cans to resell. Severe poverty has forced them into this nightmarish occupation.

Other forms of modern-day slavery include children who are forcibly taken from their families to work as soldiers, carry guns, and go into dangerous battles. In the mid-2000s, UNICEF estimated that 300,000 children under the age of 18 were being used in armed conflicts around the world; some of them were as young as seven or eight. Children, as well as adults, are traded as slaves in the commercial sex industry. In a disturbing statistic, more than 2 million children are exploited for commercial sex every year, according to the U.S. State Department's 2008 *Trafficking in Persons Report.*

Like Tubman and Douglass, Mani did not simply enjoy her freedom once she stepped onto free soil. She began to fight to stop slavery for others. Mani filed suit in a regional African court against her country for not upholding and enforcing its own laws and for denying her freedom. In October 2008, she won her case. "I knew that this was the only way to protect my child from suffering the same fate as myself. Nobody deserves to be enslaved,"[9] she told *Time* magazine. In 2009, *Time* named the 25-year-old Mani as one of the World's 100 Most Influential People. That same year, she also received the Secretary of State's Award for International Women of Courage. She met First Lady Michelle Obama and Secretary of State Hillary Clinton in Washington, D.C, at the awards ceremony.

Mani is one of the most visible warriors against slavery, which continues throughout the world, but especially in Asia and Africa. Many other individuals and organizations are working tirelessly to end slavery once and for all. A leading antislavery expert, Kevin Bales, president of Free the Slaves and the author of *Disposable People: New Slavery in a Global*

Economy, points out that the global economy does not rely on slavery. In contrast, the nineteenth-century American South needed unpaid labor to support its large-scale agricultural economy. Today it is the private business owner or entrepreneur who profits from slave labor, so that nations would not suffer economically if slavery were eradicated. He urges the public to commit to wiping out slavery and governments to renew efforts to enforce antislavery laws and not ignore these most vulnerable citizens. Bales believes that ending slavery once and for all will not take a lot of money, only a strong and dedicated will. Still, it is no simple task. To end slavery also means providing impoverished people with the tools to support themselves so that they have better alternatives and choices in their lives. Basic steps such as a village learning how to form credit unions and organize its own micro-businesses can mean big changes, according to Bales.

Supriya Awasthi is one of the activists, sometimes called "liberators," with Free the Slaves in India. She is the South Asia director of the organization. One place where Awasthi has worked is Harghad, a village in the state of Uttar Pradesh where the people have been enslaved for generations as stone breakers. Year after year, no matter how hard they worked, they remained in debt to contractors representing the mine owners. The villagers' dream has been to get their own mining leases so that they can work and earn money for themselves. Awasthi has organized them so that they can find ways to stand up to the contractors and assert their rights. "Our goal was to enable the people of Harghad to gain freedom not just on paper, not just for a day, but to enable them to live in a state of sustainable freedom forever and for everybody, " Awasthi said in an interview on the Free the Slaves Web site. She and the villagers have had some success, but still have a ways to go. "Our dream is to save money and buy a truck for the group," one villager said. "We have always loaded trucks for the contractors. Once we have our own truck, we will be self-sufficient."[10]

According to Anti-Slavery International, about 20 million people will be the victims of bonded labor, a practice in which employers give high-interest loans that can never be paid off by workers and their families. Guarani Indians in Bolivia, like this family above, are forced to live on the owners' land and work in the owners' fields for very little pay. The owners deduct money from their pay for rent and food, resulting in the Guaranis actually owing money to the owners. The Guaranis are kept as debt slaves for generations.

Once in danger of fading into history, the Underground Railroad continues to inspire people to take action to combat slavery and promote human rights. Defeating slavery in the twenty-first century means not forgetting what happened before. One night in 2002, two college seniors at Brown University were talking about the Underground Railroad and the abolitionist movement in the nineteenth century. Katherine Chon and Derek Ellerman began to wonder about modern-day slavery. As they searched the Internet for more information, they were shocked to discover the scope of human trafficking and slavery.

They learned of six Korean women who had been trafficked into prostitution in Rhode Island and forced to work in massage parlors. The women were living not far from the Brown campus in Providence when they were arrested and deported. The two students decided to try to help end slavery and human trafficking. In 2002, Chon and Ellerman founded the nonprofit organization Polaris Project, named for the North Star that guided the slaves to freedom. The project provides emergency shelter and other assistance to victims of human trafficking and slavery. These young people are the future of the fight against slavery. Like Frederick Douglass and Harriet Tubman and Hadizatou Mani, who have experienced slavery, they are determined to make sure that horrific institution, once and for all, fades into history.

CHRONOLOGY

1619	Africans are brought to Jamestown as indentured servants.
1775	First abolitionist society is founded in Philadelphia.
1788	U.S. Constitution fails to outlaw slavery.
1790s	Quaker Isaac T. Hopper helps fugitive slaves in Philadelphia.
1793	Eli Whitney's cotton gin increases the demand for slave labor.
1808	International slave trade ends in the United States.
1818	Frederick Augustus Washington Bailey (Frederick Douglass) is born in Maryland.
circa 1822	Araminta Ross, later known as Harriet Tubman, is born in Maryland.
1830s	The term *Underground Railroad* is used for the growing network aiding fugitive slaves.
1831	Nat Turner leads slave revolt in Virginia.
	William Lloyd Garrison starts his antislavery newspaper, *The Liberator*.
1838	Frederick Douglass escapes from slavery.
1840s	The Reverend John Rankin's house in Ripley, Ohio, is a safe house for fugitives crossing the Ohio River.
1848	Quaker station master Thomas Garrett is tried for aiding fugitive slaves.
1849	Harriet Tubman escapes from slavery; Henry "Box" Brown escapes from slavery in a box.

1850   The Fugitive Slave Act, requiring all citizens to aid in capturing fugitive slaves, is passed; Harriet Tubman makes her first rescue on the Underground Railroad.

1852   Harriet Beecher Stowe's *Uncle Tom's Cabin* is published.

1857   U.S. Supreme Court decides in the *Dred Scott* case that blacks cannot be citizens and that Congress cannot ban slavery in any territory.

1859   Abolitionist John Brown seizes federal armory in Harpers Ferry, Virginia.

1861   Abraham Lincoln takes office as president; the Civil War begins.

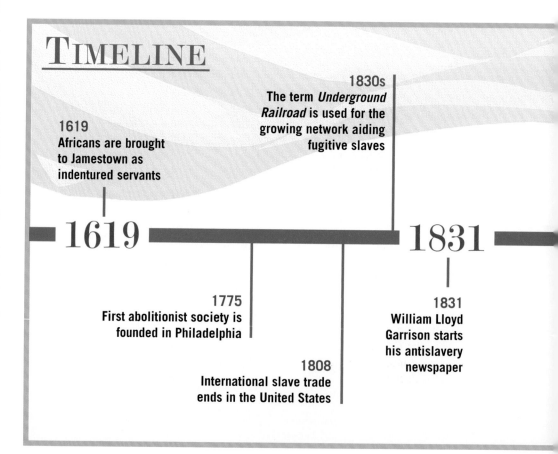

TIMELINE

1830s
The term *Underground Railroad* is used for the growing network aiding fugitive slaves

1619
Africans are brought to Jamestown as indentured servants

1619

1831

1775
First abolitionist society is founded in Philadelphia

1831
William Lloyd Garrison starts his antislavery newspaper

1808
International slave trade ends in the United States

1863   The Emancipation Proclamation frees slaves in
        Confederate states.

1865   Civil War ends; President Lincoln is assassinated; the
        Thirteenth Amendment abolishes slavery.

1895   Frederick Douglass dies on February 20 in
        Washington, D.C.

1913   Harriet Tubman dies of pneumonia on March 10 in
        Auburn, New York.

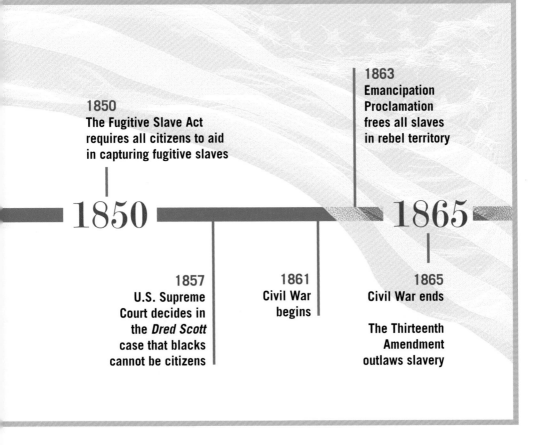

1850
The Fugitive Slave Act
requires all citizens to aid
in capturing fugitive slaves

1863
Emancipation
Proclamation
frees all slaves
in rebel territory

1850

1865

1857
U.S. Supreme
Court decides in
the *Dred Scott*
case that blacks
cannot be citizens

1861
Civil War
begins

1865
Civil War ends

The Thirteenth
Amendment
outlaws slavery

NOTES

CHAPTER 1

1. Frederick Douglass, *Narrative of the Life of Frederick Douglass.* Boston: Anti-Slavery Office, No 25 Cornhill, 1845, p. 83. Available online. URL: http://docsouth.unc.edu/neh/douglass/menu.html.

2. "Danger of Insurrection," *Staunton Spectator.* Nov. 29, 1859, p. 2. Available online. URL: http://www2.vcdh.virginia.edu/teaching/vclassroom/proslavewsht1.html.

3. Henry David Thoreau, "A Plea for Captain John Brown, October 30, 1859." Available online. URL: http://avalon.law.yale.edu/19th_century/thoreau_001.asp.

4. Fergus M. Bordewich, *Bound for Canaan: The Underground Railroad and the War for the Soul of America.* New York: Amistad, 2005, p. 4.

5. Douglass, *Narrative of the Life of Frederick Douglass*, p. 15.

6. Frederick Douglass, *My Bondage and My Freedom.* New York and Auburn: Miller, Orton & Mulligan, 1855, p. 336. Available online. URL: http://docsouth.unc.edu/neh/douglass55/douglass55.html.

7. Douglass, *Narrative of the Life of Frederick Douglass*, p. 101.

8. Ibid., pp. 107–108.

CHAPTER 2

1. Olaudah Equiano, *The Interesting Narrative of the Life of Olaudah Equiano, or Gustavus Vassa, the African.* London: G. Vassa, 1789, p. 79. Available online. URL: http://docsouth.unc.edu/neh/equiano1/menu.html.

2. "Excerpts from Massachusetts Body of Liberties." Available online. URL: http://www.constitution.org/bcp/mabodlib.txt.

3. William Wells Brown, *Narrative of William W. Brown, a Fugitive Slave.* Boston: Antislavery Office, 1847), pp. 15 16. Available online. URL: http://docsouth.unc.edu/neh/brown47/menu.html.

4. Wilbur H. Siebert, *The Underground Railroad: From Slavery to Freedom.* Mineola, N.Y.: Dover, 2006, p. 25.

5. Jean M. West, "Slavery and Sanctuary in Colonial Florida," Slavery in America. Available online. URL: http://www.slaveryinamerica.org/history/hs_es_florida_slavery.htm.

6. "*State v. Mann*," North Carolina History Project. Available online. URL: http://www.northcarolinahistory.org/encyclopedia/268/entry.

7. "The Somersett Case," Black Presence: Asian and Black History in Britain, 1500-1850, The National Archives, U.K. Available online. URL: http://www.nationalarchives.gov.uk/pathways/blackhistory/rights/docs/state_trials.htm.

8. Lord Dunmore's Proclamation. Available online. URL: http://

www.pbs.org/wgbh/aia/part2/
2narr4.html.

9. "U.S. Constitution: Article IV."
The Avalon Project Web site.
Available online. URL: http://
avalon.law.yale.edu/18th_
century/art4.asp.

10. Bordewich, *Bound for Canaan*,
p. 53.

11. Ibid., p. 51.

CHAPTER 3

1. Siebert, *The Underground Railroad*, p. 45.

2. Ibid., p. 57.

3. Levi Coffin, *Reminiscences of Levi
Coffin*. Cincinnati: Robert Clarke
& Co., 1880, p. 183. Available
online. URL: http://docsouth.
unc.edu/nc/coffin/coffin.html.

4. Douglass, *Narrative of the Life of
Frederick Douglass*, p. 41.

5. Siebert, *The Underground Railroad*, p. 26.

6. Henry Bibb, *Narrative of the Life
and Adventures of Henry Bibb,
an American Slave, Written by
Himself*. New York: Published
by the Author, 1849, pp. 13–14.
Available online. URL: http://
docsouth.unc.edu/neh/bibb/
menu.html.

7. Deborah Gray White, "Simple
Truths: Antebellum Slavery in
Black and White," *Passages to
Freedom* (edited by David W.
Blight). New York: Harper Col-
lins/Smithsonian Books, 2006,
p. 33.

8. Bordewich, *Bound for Canaan*,
p. 111.

9. William Lloyd Garrison, *The
Liberator*, January 1, 1831.
Available online. URL: http://

www.pbs.org/wgbh/aia/part4/
4h2928t.html.

10. William Lloyd Garrison, *The
Abolitionist: Or Record of the
New England Anti-Slavery
Society*. Boston: Garrison and
Knapp, 1833, p. 30. Available
online. URL: http://books.
google.com/books?id=JK0S
AAAAYAAJ&printsec=titlep
age&source=gbs_navlinks_
s#v=onepage&q=&f=false.

11. Thomas R. Gray, *The Confes-
sions of Nat Turner: The Leader
of the Late Insurrection in Southampton, Virginia*. Baltimore:
Lucas & Deaver, 1831, p. 11.
Available online. URL: http://
docsouth.unc.edu/neh/turner/
menu.html.

12. White, "Simple Truths," p. 65.

13. William Still, *The Underground
Railroad*, Philadelphia: Porter
and Coates, 1872, p. 81. Available online. URL: http://www.
quinnipiac.edu/other/abl/etext/
ugrr/ugrr.html.

CHAPTER 4

1. Sarah H. Bradford, *Scenes in the
Life of Harriet Tubman*, Auburn,
N.Y.: W.J. Moses, 1869, p. 11.
Available online. URL: http://doc
south.unc.edu/neh/bradford/
menu.html.

2. Benjamin Drew, *A North-Side
View of Slavery. The Refugees:
Narratives of Fugitive Slaves in
Canada*. Boston: J.P. Jewitt &
Co., 1854, p. 30.

3. Sarah H. Bradford, *Harriet, the
Moses of Her People*, New York:
George Lockwood & Son, 1886,
pp. 24–25. Available online.

URL: http://docsouth.unc.edu/neh/harriet/menu.html.

4. Still, *The Underground Railroad,* p. 172.

5. Bradford, *Harriet, the Moses of Her People,* p. 29.

6. Bradford, *Scenes in the Life of Harriet Tubman,* p. 19.

7. Bradford, *Harriet, the Moses of Her People,* pp. 29–30.

8. Bradford, *Scenes in the Life of Harriet Tubman,* p. 19.

9. Still, *The Underground Railroad,* p. 531.

10. Bradford, *Harriet, the Moses of Her People,* p. 53.

11. Bradford, *Harriet, the Moses of Her People,* pp. 34–35.

12. "The North Star," American Treasures of the Library of Congress. Available online. URL: http://www.loc.gov/exhibits/treasures/trr085.html.

13. Bradford, *Harriet, the Moses of Her People,* pp. 37–38.

14. Douglass, *My Bondage and My Freedom,* p. 215.

15. , Ibid., p. 279.

16. Ibid., p. 99.

17. Bordewich, *Bound for Canaan,* p. 244.

18. Ibid., p. 247.

19. Frederick Douglass letter to Harriet Tubman, August 29, 1868, published in *Harriet, the Moses of Her People* (1886) by Sarah H. Bradford, p. 135.

CHAPTER 5

1. Siebert, *The Underground Railroad,* pp. 312–313.

2. Ibid., pp. 315–316.

3. Deuteronomy 23:15. *The Holy Bible, King James Version.* Avail-

able online. URL: http://www.ebible.org/bible/kjv/.

4. Siebert, *The Underground Railroad,* p. 316.

5. Douglass, *My Bondage and My Freedom,* pp. 449–450.

6. Still, The Underground Railroad, p. 747.

7. Abraham Lincoln, "Speech on the Repeal of the Missouri Compromise," Peoria, Illinois, October 16, 1854. Available online. URL: http://www.ashbrook.org/library/19/lincoln/peoria.html.

CHAPTER 6

1. Ann Hagedorn, *Beyond the River: The Untold Story of the Heroes of the Underground Railroad,* New York: Simon & Schuster, 2002, p. 12.

2. Quoted in George and Willene Hendrick, editors, *Fleeing for Freedom: Stories of the Underground Railroad as told by Levi Coffin and William Still.* Chicago: Ivan R. Dee, 2004), p. ix.

3. Bordewich, *Bound for Canaan,* p. 199.

4. Hagedorn, *Beyond the River,* p. 83.

5. Coffin, *Reminiscences of Levi Coffin,* p. 112.

6. Ibid., p. 11.

7. Ibid., p. 112.

8. Ibid., p. 149.

9. "Today in History," Library of Congress: American Memory Web site. Available online. URL: http://memory.loc.gov/ammem/today/jun05.html.

10. "Constitution of the Commonwealth of Massachusetts." Avail-

able online. URL: http://www.
mass.gov/legis/const.htm.

11. "Virtual American Biographies:
Dred Scott." Available online.
URL: http://www.famous
americans.net/dredscott/.

12. John Brown's speech, *Africans
in America*, PBS. Viewed online.
URL: http://www.pbs.org/wgbh/
aia/part4/4p1550.html.

13. Henry David Thoreau, "A Plea
for Captain John Brown, October 30, 1859." Available online.
URL: http://avalon.law.yale.edu/
19th_century/thoreau_001.asp.

CHAPTER 7

1. Alexander H. Stephens, "Cornerstone Speech," March 21,
1861, Savannah, Georgia. Available online. URL: http://teach-
ingamericanhistory.org/library/
index.asp?documentprint=76.

2. Robert Smalls: Official Website
and Information Center. Available online. URL: http://www.
robertsmalls.org/about.htm.

3. Ibid.

4. Frederick Douglass, "Nemesis,"
Douglass' Monthly, May 1861,
collected in *Frederick Douglass:
Selected Speeches and Writ-
ings*, edited by Philip S. Foner.
Chicago: Lawrence Hill Books,
1999, p. 451.

5. Frederick Douglass, *Life and
Times of Frederick Douglass: His
Early Life as a Slave, His Escape
from Bondage, and His Complete
History to the Present Time*, Hartford, Conn.: Park Publishing,
1881, p. 358. Available online.
URL: http://docsouth.unc.edu/
neh/dougl92/menu.html.

6. "Emancipation Proclamation,"
Featured Documents: National
Archives and Records Administration Web site. Available online.
URL: http://www.archives.gov/
exhibits/featured_documents/
emancipation_proclamation/
transcript.html.

7. Letter from Abraham Lincoln
to A.G. Hodges, "If Slavery Is
Not Wrong, Nothing Is Wrong,"
American Treasures of the
Library of Congress. Available
online. URL: http://www.loc.
gov/exhibits/treasures/trt027.
html.

8. "Georgia and the Confederacy,
1865," *The American Historical
Review*, Vol. 1, No. 1 (October
1895), p. 97. Available online.
URL: http://www.jstor.org/pss/
1834020.

9. "The Assassination," *New York
Times*, April 17, 1865, p. 1. Available online. URL: http://query.
nytimes.com/mem/archive-free/
pdf?res=9E00EED91F30EE34BC
4052DFB266838E679FDE.

10. "The United States Constitution:
Amendment 13." Available online. URL: http://www.usconsti-
tution.net/const.html#Am13.

CHAPTER 8

1. "Martin Luther King Jr.: 'I Have
a Dream,'" American Rhetoric
Web site. Available online. URL:
http://www.americanrhetoric.
com/speeches/mlkihaveadream.
htm.

2. Larry Gara, *The Liberty Line:
The Legend of the Underground
Railroad*, Lexington: University
of Kentucky Press, 1996, p. 2.

3. Kate Clifford Larson, Underground Railroad Research Forum. Available online. URL: http://afrigeneas.com/forum-ugrr/index.cgi?md=read:id=278.

4. Fergus Bordewich, "History's Tangled Threads," *The New York Times*, Feb. 2, 2007. Available online. URL: http://www.nytimes.com/2007/02/02/opinion/02bordewich.html.

5. "The Wellman Scale," Friends of the Underground Railroad. Available online. URL: http://fourr.org/future_wellmanscale.html.

6. Timothy Williams, "Why Is Harriet Tubman Facing South?" *The New York Times*, Nov. 13, 2008. Available online. URL: http://cityroom.blogs.nytimes.com/2008/11/13/why-is-harriet-tubman-facing-south.

7. Mangoa Mosota, "No Woman Should Suffer the Way I Did," *The Standard*, June 28, 2009. Available online. URL: http://www.eastandard.net/mag/InsidePage.php?id=1144017987&cid=499&.

8. "Breaking the Silence: Beating the Drum," United Nations Web site. Available online. http://www.un.org/en/slavery/sg-message.shtml.

9. Zainab Salbi, "Hadizatou Mani," *Time*, May 11, 2009, p. 112.

10. "In Their Own Words—Supriya Awasthi," Free the Slaves. Available online. URL: http://www.freetheslaves.net/Page.aspx?pid=465.

BIBLIOGRAPHY

Africans in America, PBS. Available online. URL: http://www. pbs.org/wgbh/aia/home.html.

Blight, David W. *Passages to Freedom: The Underground Railroad in History and Memory*. New York: Smithsonian Institution/ HarperCollins, 2006.

Bordewich, Fergus M. *Bound for Canaan: The Underground Railroad and the War for the Soul of America*. New York: Amistad, 2005.

Clinton, Catherine. *Harriet Tubman: The Road to Freedom*. New York: Little, Brown & Company, Back Bay Books, 2004.

Coffin, Levi. *Reminiscences of Levi Coffin*. Cincinnati: Robert Clark & Co., 1880. Available online. URL: http://docsouth. unc.edu/nc/coffin/coffin.html.

Douglass, Frederick. *Life and Times of Frederick Douglass: His Early Life as a Slave, His Escape from Bondage, and His Complete History to the Present Time*. Hartford, Conn.: Park Publishing, 1881. Available online. URL: http://docsouth.unc. edu/neh/dougl92/menu.html.

———. *My Bondage and My Freedom*. New York and Auburn: Miller, Orton & Mulligan, 1855. Available online. URL: http://docsouth.unc.edu/neh/douglass55/douglass55.html.

———. *Narrative of the Life of Frederick Douglass*. Boston: Anti-Slavery Office, No 25 Cornhill, 1845. Available online. URL: http://docsouth.unc.edu/neh/douglass/menu.html.

"Exploring a Common Past: Researching and Interpreting the Underground Railroad." National Park Service. Available online. URL: http://www.nps.gov/history/history/online_ books/ugrr/exugrr1.htm.

Gara, Larry. *The Liberty Line: The Legend of the Underground Railroad.* Lexington: University of Kentucky Press, 1996.

Hagedorn, Ann. *Beyond the River: The Untold Story of the Heroes of the Underground Railroad.* New York: Simon & Schuster, 2002.

Hendrick, George and Willene, eds. *Fleeing for Freedom: Stories of the Underground Railroad as told by Levi Coffin and William Still.* Chicago: Ivan R. Dee, 2004.

Larson, Kate Clifford. *Bound for the Promised Land: Harriet Tubman, Portrait of an American Hero.* New York: Ballantine Books, 2003.

———. "Harriet Tubman Biography." Available online. URL: http://www.harriettubmanbiography.com.

Passage to Freedom. "Discovering Ohio's Underground Railroad History." Available online. URL: http://passagetofreedomohio. org. Robert Smalls: Official Website and Information Center. Available online. URL: http://www.robertsmalls.org/about.htm.

Rose, P.K. "Black Dispatches: Black American Contributions to Union Intelligence During the Civil War." Available online. URL: https://www.cia.gov/library/center-for-the-study-of-intelligence/csi-publications/books-and-monographs/black-dispatches/index.html.

Siebert, Wilbur H. *The Underground Railroad: From Slavery to Freedom.* Mineola, N.Y.: Dover, 2006.

Stanley, Campbell W. *The Slave Catchers: Enforcement of the Fugitive Slave Law, 1850–1860.* New York: W.W. Norton, 1972.

"Steal Away, Steal Away . . .": A Guide to the Underground Railroad in New Jersey. New Jersey Historical Commission. Available online. URL: http://www.njstatelib.org/digit/h673/h6732002.pdf.

Still, William. *The Underground Railroad.* Philadelphia: Porter & Coates, 1872. Available online. URL: http://www.quinnipiac. edu/other/ABL/etext/ugrr/ugrrmain.html.

Strausbaugh, John S. "On the Trail of Brooklyn's Underground Railroad." *The New York Times,* October 12, 2007.

The Underground Railroad in Virginia. Available online. URL: http://www.racetimeplace.com/ugrr/index.htm.

Further Reading

BOOKS

Calkhoven, Laurie. *Harriet Tubman: Leading the Way to Freedom.* New York: Sterling, 2008.

Fradin, Dennis Brindell. *My Family Shall Be Free! The Life of Peter Still.* New York: Harper Collins Publishers, 2001.

Hendrick, George and Hendrick, Willene, editors. *Fleeing for Freedom: Stories of the Underground Railroad as told by Levi Coffin and William Still.* Chicago: Ivan R. Dee, 2004.

Parker, John P. *His Promised Land: The Autobiography of John P. Parker, Former Slave and Conductor on the Underground Railroad,* ed. Stuart Seely Sprague. New York: W.W. Norton, 1996.

Ricks, Mary Kay. *Escape on the Pearl: The Heroic Bid for Freedom on the Underground Railroad.* New York: Harper Perennial, 2008.

Robbins, Trina. *Freedom Songs: A Tale of the Underground Railroad.* Minneapolis: Stone Arch Books, 2008.

Stowe, Harriet Beecher. *Uncle Tom's Cabin.* New York: Dover, 2005.

WEB SITES

Adventure Cycling Association: Underground Railroad Bicycle Route

http://www.adventurecycling.org/ugrr

Bicyclers can learn more about the Underground Railroad by traveling the same routes taken by slaves on their journeys to freedom.

Born in Slavery: Slave Narratives from the Federal Writers' Project, 1936–1938. Library of Congress.

http://memory.loc.gov/ammem/snhtml/snhome.html

During the Great Depression, researchers with the Federal Writers' Project of the Works Progress Administration collected more than 2,300 first-person accounts of slavery and 500 photographs of former slaves. The stories in the collection provide a glimpse into the real lives of American slaves.

Free the Slaves

http://www.freetheslaves.net/Page.aspx?pid=183

Free the Slaves is a nonprofit organization in Washington, D.C., that works to end slavery around the world through education, advocacy, and intervention.

Harriet Tubman Biography

http://www.harriettubmanbiography.com

Tubman biographer Kate Clifford Larson provides timelines, biographical information, and the latest research on the famous conductor of the Underground Railroad.

In Motion: The African-American Migration Experience

http://www.inmotionaame.org/home.cfm

The Schomberg Center for Research in Black Culture provides a scholarly look at the transatlantic slave trade, the journeys of slaves on the Underground Railroad, and the sale of slaves in markets and auctions in this country.

National Geographic: The Underground Railroad

http://www.nationalgeographic.com/railroad/j1.html

This inspiring interactive site on the Underground Railroad also offers links and educational resources for students and teachers.

National Underground Railroad Freedom Center

http://www.freedomcenter.org

The cutting-edge museum in Cincinnati, Ohio, is a vital resource for information on the history of the Underground Railroad and worldwide antislavery efforts in the twenty-first century.

National Underground Railroad Network to Freedom

http://www.nps.gov/history/ugrr

Find out what the National Park Service is doing to promote the Underground Railroad on this Web site, which has the latest approaches to researching the historic era and lists federally recognized sites, including churches, safe houses, and other locations.

Passage to Freedom: Discovering Ohio's Underground Railroad History

http://passagetofreedomohio.org

Explore Ohio's history of the Underground Railroad on this site that celebrates the role of Ohioans in helping runaway slaves from the South to cross the Ohio River and settle in towns like Oberlin, Ohio, or move on to Canada.

Photo Credits

INDEX

ABOUT THE AUTHOR

While researching this book, **ANN MALASPINA** learned of Underground Railroad sites in places where she has lived. Near the neighborhood in Brooklyn, New York, where she was born, the Bridge Street African Methodist Episcopal Wesleyan Church was a safe haven for runaway slaves before the Civil War. In central Ohio where she attended Kenyon College, fugitive slaves found a network of freed blacks and white abolitionists who helped them get to Canada. Now Ann lives not far from David L. Holden's house in Jersey City, New Jersey. An amateur astronomer, Holden used his observatory to receive and send signals about runaway slaves, whom he hid in his basement. Ann hopes this book will inspire readers to learn about Underground Railroad history in places where they live and travel.